RIDING THE WHITE WATER RAPIDS

Career Success in the 21st Century

Dear Ms. Nooyi

Wishing you continued success in the White Water Rapids,

Lots of Fulfillment and Joy

Ayalla

Ayalla Reuven-Lelong

RIDING THE WHITE WATER RAPIDS

Career Success in the 21st Century

Ayalla Reuven-Lelong

RIDING THE WHITE WATER RAPIDS
Career Success In the 21st Century

Senior Editors & Producers: Contento
Translator: Ilan Reuven-Lelong
Editor: Ilan Reuven-Lelong
Cover and Book Design: Liliya Lev Ari

Copyright © 2015 by Ayalla Reuven-Lelong and Contento

All rights reserved. No part of this book may be translated, reproduced, stored in a retrieval system or transmitted, in any form or by any means, electronic, photocopying, recording or otherwise, without prior permission in writing from the author and publisher.

ISBN: 978-965-550-250-3

International sole distributor: Contento
22 Isserles Street, 6701457, Tel Aviv, Israel
www.ContentoNow.com
Semrik10@gmail.com

*To my beloved parents and precious daughter Lior
who taught me what unconditional love is*

Table of Contents

- *Preface: My Personal Journey* 9
- *Acknowledgements* 15
1. *Setting Out for the Journey: Rowing in White Water* ... 17
2. *Mindset Land* 53
3. *Whole Brain Land* 77
4. *EQ Land* 100
5. *Centered Leadership Land* 134
6. *I-21* 160
7. *Back to Work* 169
- *Q&A: Theoretical Background for Success in the 21st Century* 178
    - Mindset Land 179
    - Whole Brain Land 199
    - EQ Land 217
    - Centered Leadership Land 239
- *I Have a Dream* 256
- *Sources* 259

Preface:
My Personal Journey

My journey began about 15 years ago, when I first held Daniel Goleman's book about *Emotional Intelligence*. My interest in this field started from an understanding that our success does not rely on our cognitive and professional skills alone – an important part of it relies on skills of a different kind. This understanding led me to explore the essence of success of managers and employees in the 21st century.

Since then, I have been certified as an evaluator of emotional intelligence. I founded a center for the measurement, evaluation and development of emotional intelligence in businesses and organizations and developed expertise in building and implementing related organizational strategies. I now lead strategic change processes for large companies in Israel: analyzing the challenges, assessing the executives' soft skills, and building a plan to help them cope with these challenges. In addition, I design and conduct workshops, lecture at conventions and participate in professional panels.

As I meet with dozens of executives each month, I sense that most of them lack a real understanding as to where the organizational world is heading. As someone who sits through organizational meetings for long hours, I frequently witness the extent to which top managements strive to find talented executives of all ranks to promote, and the difficulties they experience.

Surprisingly, it turns out that over 70 percent of appointments or promotions in organizations are compromises. The 20th century classic and first choice candidate – a professional prodigy, a wizard – often fails in leading his employees, in retaining customers or adapting to changes. A second candidate, who has excellent relationships with employees, fails to offer significant value propositions to his customers, while a third candidate who displays high soft skills and excellent interactions with both employees and customers, lacks adequate professional skills.

It should be noted that this scenario is not found only in management, but in many other fields as well. The change derives from the fact that professional requirements are changing and expanding to areas where acquired studies and accumulated experience and skills are insufficient. The "organizational topography" that has developed over the past 10 years is dramatically different from the one we knew in the past, and it might change even further in the next few years. Today, in such an organizational reality, employees and executives are required to have a far more complex range of skills. Unfortunately, those who do not internalize this reality will find themselves irrelevant to the organizations they work in. In the best case scenario, even in spite of their hard efforts, they will lag behind while others pass them by. Eventually, they might even find themselves outside the workforce.

My private journey to understand the elements of career success in the 21st century sharpened and peaked during the past five years. This journey provided me with the insight that success in the 21st century will belong to those who think and act differently from the way they did in the 20th century. While it was previously common knowledge that graduating from a good university with high grades would ensure a better future for us and for our children, we now realize that university is simply a prerequisite but is surely insufficient to guarantee success.

As a consultant, it wasn't easy for me to see talented individuals become stagnant in their careers, not knowing how and why they got there. I felt great frustration and sadness in the face of this reality. I understood that these employees and executives would need a new and updated roadmap in order to succeed, since the map they were using did not serve them anymore. I also realized that in order to successfully lead the executives whom I work with toward success, I must understand the most important factors for their ongoing success.

Throughout my journey, I delved into the leading research and professional literature on this subject. I studied the various models and applied them to the daily practice in different organizations. I met and had conversations with hundreds of senior and junior executives through lectures and personal meetings. Eventually, these led me to the understanding of what are the most important competencies and skills that distinguish between those who are capable managers in the gushing "white water" from those who are not.

By the end of my own journey, my conclusion was that success in the 21st century will be achieved by those who become acquainted with four key ideas, which are represented in this book by four lands. Wise use of the principles and insights presented in each land will enable an individual to create his own fifth land – the land of success.

The objective of this book is, therefore, to equip the reader with an updated roadmap for success, by means of experiencing a journey to five lands. Each land fulfills an important role in paving the way. The roadmap is represented through a simple spiral model, where every step is based on the previous one and plays a significant role in the journey – a model which I have introduced and implemented with managements and executives of all ranks, in various organizations in Israel.

The reader will experience this model through the journey that the protagonist undergoes to those five conceptual lands.

The first part of the book is the story of a classic talented and ambitious junior executive named Michael. Although he excels professionally, he is forced to realize that the times are indeed changing. Following an annual feedback meeting, Michael is suddenly confronted with the reality that he must make a different kind of effort in order to maintain a continued successful career.

For continuous success, he has to go through an exceptional adventure. He then sets out on an unusual journey, escorted by an intelligent, pleasant and assertive consultant, Rona, who will guide him to the five lands. In each land, he will meet different people, some of them quite strange and surreal. Through these experiences, he will gather insights that are significant to his continued success in the 21st century.

The second part of the book contains questions for thought and reflection, in addition to numerous theories and research upon which the book chapters are based.

It is important to emphasize that even though the protagonist of the story is an executive, this book is also intended for employees who are not managers and are not interested in a management position. It is intended for all those who are interested in recognition and success in their careers, while enjoying life to the fullest, including family, friends and leisure.

You can simply read the story or delve deeply into the theoretical part. Either way, I wish you the best of luck in your personal journey.

***

Like those white water rapids that illustrate today's reality, the concepts covered in this book evolve faster than we can write about them – the journey to success and fulfillment is a never-ending adventure. I will be happy to have your feedback on this book: suggestions, questions or comments. You are welcome to write to me at success.i21@eq-el.co.il.

Acknowledgements

I would like to acknowledge all those who helped me during my personal journey and made the writing of this book possible. Most of all I would like to acknowledge all the executives whom I had the privilege to accompany during the last few years. Openly and dedicatedly, they enabled me to gain those valuable insights into the quest for success in this radically dynamic reality that we are currently experiencing.

Special thanks to **Eran Shalev** (senior partner, KPMG Israel) who, through his special approach and personality, challenged me and enabled me to learn and understand the complexity of the management world in the 21st century.

Thanks to **Dr. Niva Dolev**, my friend and partner, for her infinite availability, depth, insight, encouragement, empathy and support.

Heartfelt thanks to **Dr. Tzippi Blumenfeld**, for her professional support, for her constant desire to assist and help.

Special thanks to my spouse, **Ilan**, who is always with me, letting me believe that the sky is the limit. Thank you for your infinite giving, special way of thinking, questions and profound insights.

I wish to thank all those whose ideas and models are described in this book. Much effort was made to avoid reproduction of copyrighted material and to present these works in a manner that constitutes fair use. Above all, I hope this book reflects my great appreciation of these works. I encourage readers to delve further and read the cited sources, as they are all essential readings for anyone interested in succeeding in the 21st century.

Ayalla Reuven-Lelong, March 2015

1
Setting Out for the Journey: Rowing in White Water

Annual Feedback

The seeds of this journey were sown during an annual feedback session with my boss, John, in his spacious office on the executive floor. I remember the conversation and all that followed in great detail. Mostly, I remember myself looking sideways – checking to see if, perhaps, there was another person in the room; he simply couldn't be talking about me...

John was an extraordinary leader. Like similar managers in our company, he was highly focused on his mission. Unlike them, he didn't focus exclusively on the bottom line of the profit and loss statement. It was important to him to understand each team member's thinking process and to encourage our creativity. It was especially important to him to conduct an in-depth personal feedback session with each of us.

Formally, all executives were supposed to conduct such a

conversation. But in fact, this wasn't always done, and even when it was, the feedback was usually superficial. It was clear that they didn't really believe in the feedback and mostly considered it a waste of precious time, taking us away from the many tasks we already had.

But John had to be different: he spoke of what he called "the process." He said that he considered himself responsible for leading each and every one of us to realize our abilities to the fullest, acting as a kind of mentor. Sounds good, doesn't it? But you can take my word for it that back then, I would have gladly passed on such an opportunity. All I wanted was a quiet work environment that enabled me to prove myself and continue with my product development.

Just like previous feedback conversations, this one also began by focusing on professional and technical points. The beginning was indeed promising: John complimented me on my expertise and high-level of performance, affirmatively mentioning my managerial abilities and my ability to meet deadlines. But those moments of grace quickly passed as the conversation moved on to a full description of the issues that were holding me back, accompanied by suggestions and details as to my options…

He began by mentioning a specific example: "Do you remember what happened two months ago with Tami?" he said. "She had to go back home to be with her daughter, who had the flu. When she told you she had to leave, she also mentioned the measures she took to make sure that her team would be able to manage without her. Your reaction was harsh and without empathy. You made her leave in tears as you implied that she wasn't really committed to her job if she neglected her team and compromised the project's deadline."

I wanted to tell him that he got the whole thing wrong and that he didn't hear my side of the story. But he continued. "Also, during the last project, when we had to work hand-in-hand with teams from the UK and Germany, the project manager asked to replace you. He claimed that you couldn't get along with the other participants and that you let everyone feel that your way was the only way. No one was really sorry when he announced that you weren't part of the team anymore…

"Six months ago," he continued, "Roy led an organizational strategic change which, according to him, was essential to our value proposition and ability to keep on thriving as an organization." Yes, indeed, I remembered when Roy, our CEO, just came back from a convention with some new bright ideas.

"Well, you repeatedly expressed your firm objection to this program. You didn't even give it a chance, or really try to understand it. Instead, you provided everyone with plenty of reasons to object it. You kept on describing the existing state in bright colors and as much better than it really was, as if there was no reason for a change. All along the way, neither the opinion you expressed nor your behavior demonstrated that you were open to any change."

John kept talking in terms of open-mindedness, interpersonal skills, adaptability to new situations, creativity and emotional intelligence. I remember telling myself: here comes the gibberish part as always, and with it comes the end of our meeting… Just a few more minutes of silence and random nodding on my account – and I would be safely out.

I wasn't the only member of our team who was deterred by terms such as "soft skills," with all their "touchy-feely" connotations. Most of us thought that the introduction of emotional concepts into a "hard skills" organization like ours is a conspiracy by less talented individuals who couldn't find a more dignified way to make a living.

This time though, things didn't move as smoothly as I had expected, when John turned to me and said, "Michael, you are a real challenge for me. I truly think you have high professional skills. But, as far as adaptability, creativity and interpersonal skills are concerned, you are completely clueless. Honestly, throughout the period you have been working here, I haven't seen any progress, not even the beginning of a process, in the areas related to your emotional intelligence. Therefore, it appears that I'm unable to promote you to your next managerial position. I suggest that you schedule a meeting with Martha. Talk to her and see how we should proceed."

Once again, I doubted he was talking to me because I wasn't used to hearing my name next to the words "no progress" or "no process." After all, I was the only one in my MA class who graduated with the highest distinction. I was always highly sought-after in my field, and everyone around me considered me "successful." John himself said that he always chose me for the most complex technical assignments, because it was clear to him that if anyone could overcome the difficulty, **I would be the one.**

So where did this whole "unable to promote you" thing come from? How is the whole story of interpersonal skills related to me? After all, I didn't come to work here as an elementary school teacher or a social worker.

And yet, recently, I did miss out on two promotion opportunities, even though everyone knew that professionally speaking, I was the most competent candidate. To be honest, looking back to my previous job, I hadn't been promoted according to my expectations. For months, I had this feeling that my career wasn't progressing as well as it should have... So, what was it that I did not understand?

John continued, "Michael, you are important to me on a personal level. That's why I have to tell you that as a part of your job you also have a duty to develop your soft skills and a unique value proposition. You must do this in order to become indispensable to the organization and to be someone who won't be easy to replace. This is the approach that guides me at work.

"You know, it's relatively easy to find people who will do the job. But it's definitely much harder to find people with flexibility of thought and action, who know how to be effective team players, and who can lead others in such a complex and changing reality. You need to understand that we can no longer afford mediocre employees and executives. In order to be ahead of our competition we must employ highly-qualified people, with emphasis on both professional and soft skills. Unfortunately, nowadays there is nowhere to escape to and nowhere to hide. If you fail to develop these skills, I'm afraid we'll have to pass over you in the next promotion round as well.

"For the future of our organization, we need executives who are capable of leading a change, who work well in teams, who promote their employees' development and provide an extraordinary service offering and value proposition to their customers. I've tried to tell you this many times in the past, but I feel that my words fell on deaf ears."

I left the room quite confused, like I had been spoken to in a foreign language that I didn't understand. I couldn't comprehend these skills that John spoke about – how to acquire them and how exactly they might advance my career. The first thought that crossed my mind was that I would be better off if I quit. Any other organization would be happy to hire a professional manager like me.

I arrived home and talked with my spouse, Mia, about the meeting I had with John and about my wish to resign. The conversation wasn't easy for me, as she implied that there might be some truth in John's words. Eventually, we concluded that I shouldn't leave my job before exhausting all the options at my disposal.

On the day following my meeting with John, the first thing I did was to call Martha, our Human Resource Manager, who is known to be sharp and understanding. I remembered the orientation and the advice she gave me when I first came to the company, which really helped me to get around and understand the balance of power within the organization. Martha was polite and to the point. "I'll be happy to meet with you," she said, "but please take into account that this is a long and in-depth process requiring time and effort, and you have to be open and willing to go through it."

"No problem," I answered, thinking that time would not be an obstacle for me. After all, I do things twice as quickly as anyone else. I thought that in two or three weeks, after one or two meetings with Martha, I would probably be in an entirely different position.

The meeting was scheduled for the next week. I was tense and nervous during the waiting time. I just wanted to get it over with. On the day of the meeting, I went up to the executive floor. Martha welcomed me with a big smile, slightly easing my fears. She offered me coffee and asked me to tell her about my expectations. I described the meeting with John, how he told me that he couldn't promote me as long as I failed to develop my soft skills, even though he recognized the fact that I was extremely talented and professional. I explained to her how confused I was: "It's inconceivable. I feel like someone has changed the rules of the game without bothering to keep me informed."

Martha listened intently and said, "Michael, you're not alone. As a Human Resource Manager, I can testify that many employees and managers, even excellent professional ones, experience frustration and disorientation. It happens in all organizations, regardless of their size and area of activity. The reason for this feeling is that indeed, the rules of the game have changed. But, notice that soft skills are not a new concept; they've been part of the organizational talk for years. What's new is that we now understand that developing such skills is a critical component in one's ability to succeed and critical for any organizations as a whole."

"So, what does it mean for me?" I asked.

"It means that, if in the past, you could coast along thanks to your high analytical abilities, which could somehow compensate for your lack of adaptability and leadership skills, and especially for your lack of interpersonal skills, this privilege doesn't exist anymore. Now, the success of employees and managers is dependent upon their ability to develop, learn, explore new areas and reinvent themselves, just as much as it depends upon their cognitive abilities and performance."

"But you and I both know that our company is very successful. Why should we change anything?" I asked.

Martha replied "Do you remember the central point of Roy's speech during the toast, last week?"

Well, actually, I didn't remember much...

"He said that the fact that the company is highly successful today doesn't imply anything about its ability to continue to be successful in the future. The most important part of his speech was the part where he turned to his executives – you and me, among others. He said that we all must be responsible for our own personal development, as this is the key that will enable us to reinvent ourselves, to create future products and services, to motivate employees with diverse backgrounds, to be an employer of choice, to differentiate ourselves from the competition and to provide a significant value proposition for our customers and potential customers, in order to be their clear choice."

I nodded. I was ashamed to admit that at that time, I thought that Roy was using rhetoric, and everything he said was meaningless to me.

Martha continued, "Michael, I had a conversation with Roy and John about you. They both think highly of you and think you are quite capable of making it through the process and becoming an executive in the 21st century. They both agreed that the organization needs to invest in you and put you through a development process."

I panicked.

What did "development process" mean? It sounded as if I was underdeveloped.

Martha noticed my reaction and smiled, "First of all, you can relax. Our company allows only those valuable and high potential managers and employees to participate in this program. You are about to receive a rare opportunity to embark on a journey that will influence your life in a deep and meaningful way. But you should know that a prerequisite to embarking on this journey is a truthful willingness and honest desire to strengthen those abilities and skills that managers need in order to succeed in a changing world such as ours."

I asked Martha for some time to consider the proposal over the weekend before giving my final answer. I left her office feeling that not only had I not gotten any answers, but that my questions and doubts had simply increased.

The thoughts going through my mind during that weekend were jolting. I got the feeling that perhaps I was in the wrong profession, living in the wrong place, at the wrong time. I thought about my father, who worked as a senior engineer for most of his life and was never required to undergo what I am going through. For decades, people had been given clear and straightforward titles. But now, just when I came along, requirements were suddenly changing. Now, in order to be promoted to the senior positions I aspired to, I had to adopt skills from an unknown strange world.

Eventually, I accepted the challenge to embark on the journey, hoping to understand the capabilities that would qualify me to become a successful manager in the 21st century.

The next conversation with Martha was short and concise. She expressed her satisfaction with my decision and handed me Rona's phone number. Rona would be my guide in what she called "The Five Lands Journey."

"I guarantee that this journey with Rona will be challenging and exciting and will open a whole new world for you. Of course, there may be moments when you would like to quit. Nevertheless, I'm sure that you are not a quitter, and you may rest assured that you won't come back the same person," she said with a wide smile.

Changing the Rules of the Game

Shortly after I returned to my office I called Rona and we scheduled a meeting. Two days later, when I entered her office, I was surprised to find a beaming woman, full of self-esteem, in her early forties. I don't know what I was expecting; I may have pictured a dreary counselor. I immediately started telling her about myself and everything I had talked about with John, going into my frustrations and asking unfocused questions.

Rona took her time before answering. She didn't take her eyes off me as I spoke, and when I was finally silent, she said both pleasantly and authoritatively, "Evidently, we have plenty of work to do…"

Wondering, I looked back at her as she continued, "Before you entered my office I went over your impressive résumé. Your professional assessments are also some of the best I've read. But it's apparent that the gap between your professional and soft skills is huge. My impression is that sitting in front of me is a guy with low self-awareness who would prefer no substantial change, so that he can go on with his familiar way of life; someone who is focused on the mission at hand and incapable of seeing the individuals around him.

"Were you aware that you never gave me a chance to introduce myself? You didn't even try to lend an ear and understand the nature and purpose of the meeting; you didn't even try to find out who your audience was in order to adapt your style of communication. In your current state, as a team manager, it appears that you are neither capable of creating a sense of trust nor can you lead changes or offer a winning value proposition. Still, here you are, telling me how surprised you are that you didn't get your promotion."

Ouch! That hurt...

"OK, go on," I answered.

"Michael, according to what I see, in the past it was obvious to you that if you went to college and got good grades, the world would be at your feet. However, if you keep on neglecting the skills which you tend to think little of, you will find that the keys to success have moved on to other hands."

What keys was she talking about?

Rona turned around and took an orange book off the shelf entitled *A Whole New Mind*, by Daniel Pink.[1]

"To me, this book is the basis of it all. It talks about change that is already happening, from the knowledge era to an era that Pink calls **the conceptual era**. The book describes the circumstances leading to the change. But, at this moment, for the matter at hand, the bottom line is that people like you, experts in information, are already unable to supply all the goods.

"Individuals and organizations striving to succeed in a reality which is changing so fast, right before our eyes, should adopt a wider approach, integrating qualities which were discarded in the past. Naturally, professional skills and technical know-how will remain central areas in any new era, but employees and executives will also require the ability to synthesize and innovate. The future belongs to those who are capable of merging different disciplines and creating meaning and real value in their doings, those who can understand others and their needs. Those who can reinvent themselves will be able to offer a compelling value proposition to the organization and its customers. Individuals who master these skills will determine the upcoming state of mind of modern life, in the workplace and in business. And you would want to be there, Michael."

I must say I didn't quite understand what the hell she was talking about, and what all this had to do with the feedback conversation with John, or with my success. However, I tried very hard to hide my feelings. Besides, the thought of the promises I had made to Mia and Martha motivated me, and I answered quickly, "OK, I'm ready, when are we going?"

Rona smiled. "Wait a minute. Before we go, we must prepare for the journey and understand what caused the change of rules. Any significant process of change begins for certain reasons."

"I am listening."

"In order to understand today's reality, we must return to the mid-18th century, when the industrial revolution began. Human society switched from manual production to industrial production and discovered the power of machines and mass production. This revolution initiated significant social and economic changes. At first, the pace of changes could be measured in terms of "half-a-century" or decades. Since then, the pace of change has continuously progressed, being the result of accelerated industrial, technological and economic development.

"Technology changed the face of modern society and economy. Industrial production brought about great wealth in terms of higher quality and lower prices of products, but also led to fierce competition. This abundance, as well as the competition, spread from the western industrialized countries to other regions of the world. The latest trend is the relocation of manufacturing to East Asia, due to the availability of cheaper manpower, further increasing the competition and operational complexity.

"As the East Asian economies grow and the reach of the Internet expands, competition further escalates. It is now commonly expected that some of the knowledge-intensive professions will also relocate, just like the manufacturing ones. Various professional services, such as accounting, law, financial management and even medicine, are already available as offshore and outsourcing services from India or China. Their quality won't be inferior to that of their colleagues in the West, but their cost will be significantly lower."

"So, why is this new?" I asked. "It's widely known that nowadays everyone is continuously competing with everyone for everything, and everywhere."

"First, remember that since the industrial revolution, the world has seen several cycles of change," Rona answered. "Eventually, accompanied by many social revolutions, these changes brought about better lives for many people in the western world and created a wealthy middle class which enjoys stable growth and even better prospects for their children. However, there are many warning signs that this time, it's going to be different.

"What is new today is that this dynamic reality has crossed a threshold – it is so intense, broad and profound that it truly is a game changer. That is to say, it brings about changes in the rules of the game and, accordingly – changes in the skills required for success.

"Today, there is a consensus that in the next few decades of the 21st century, the economy will undergo a change that hasn't been seen in the past two hundred years.

"This situation can be compared to the reality of **white water rafting**. The question is no longer whether or not we will fall, but when will it happen. Then, when we are in the water, the question is whether we can board the raft once again. Michael, you must understand that the odds are not in our favor."

"Not in our favor, in what respect?" I asked…

"Current studies show that only 30% of organizations and managers will be able to 'board the raft back' successfully, to continue using this metaphor. And even then, they will have to deal with a different reality – meaning that the raft will be in a different place. Using another metaphor for the organizational world, the one of survival – it's worth mentioning that Charles Darwin, father of the theory of evolution, didn't actually claim that the strongest, fastest or even smartest are the fittest who survive, but rather those who are best capable of adapting to their environment, especially in a changing one.

"One key factor for adaptation and survival is cooperation. Therefore, in such a changing environment as the one we are currently experiencing, each organization must see to it that the best people work together, in cooperation, guided by a common purpose and motivated by a strong value system.

"But this alone is not enough. Securing the continuity of success demands that organizations divide their resources wisely between present requirements and future needs. They must be able to perform their ongoing activities and to successfully meet the current challenges, while progressively adapting these activities to changes and to future anticipated changes... Studies show that very few can do both simultaneously."

"And what is it that enables such simultaneous performance?" I wondered.

"Organizations need leaders capable of connecting with people, viewing challenging situations in a positive light and assuming responsibility for all organizational and personal processes. This is why our abilities to adapt to changes, leave our comfort zone, develop and grow are of crucial importance for our ongoing success, both on the personal and organizational levels.

"But before you leave your own comfort zone and embark on this journey, let's go over the factors that change the rules of the game and create the white water that I was talking about."

The Factors that Change the Rules of the Game

"Look here," Rona continued, "I'm not an expert in economics and business management, but one thing is obvious to me and to everyone else: the reality we once knew is changing dramatically, and many factors are inducing this change.

"I would like to focus on seven factors which came up during in-depth interviews conducted by Steve Tappin with about 150 senior executives. Tappin is a counselor and confidant of top-notch senior executives from global organizations. He included these interviews in a book called *The Secrets of CEOs*[2] that he wrote together with economic journalist Andrew Cave, also followed by a sequel that they wrote after an additional interview round with 200 senior executives."[3]

She handed me a tablet and said, "Take it – it will accompany us on our journey. Take a look at the screen with the result of those interviews – the list of the top seven game changers. These are the major factors which are changing the rules of the game and creating the white water rafting reality."

The Rules of the Game are Changing

- Economic Crises
- Globalization
- Sustainability
- Technology
- Regulation
- Generation Y
- Competition for each Customer

1. Economic Crises

"The first factor they mentioned was **economic crises**. In the past, an economic crisis would come about every eight or 10 years. Nowadays, one crisis follows another. Every day I open the financial section and panic. Nobel Prize laureates in economics speak of a lost decade, in financial terms. In light of the massive protests and the situation in the markets of Europe and the United States, it is obvious that there aren't many reasons to be optimistic."

"I agree with you," I answered. "In terms of uncertainty and the frequency of economic crises and recoveries, it feels like we are actually rafting in white water."

"Yes, and please consider the fact that the many global changes, which are already influencing us, might affect our daily work even further. Senior executives struggle to manage in the best possible way, juggling between risks and opportunities. If, in the past, they waited for better conditions in order to act and take new initiatives, most organizations now realize that they must learn to act under constant uncertainty in order to succeed. Sure, uncertainty has always existed, but today it also affects organizations and business areas which were once immune to it."

"OK, I know about globalization, but what global changes are you talking about?"

2. Globalization

"Your question brings us to the second factor, **globalization**. It's known that the world has become a small village. Globalization influences organizations and is a major element in the depth and expansion of competition. Accordingly, it is an important game changer. In the past, globalization consisted of getting a foothold – business organizations, mostly Western, opened branches in other countries and acted as if these were just local copies of the original home branches. Today, it's impossible to act this way. Many enterprises failed because they couldn't understand local customers, local needs and the different management cultures in those emerging new markets. Those who tried to impose prices, products or Western business models, didn't realize their expectations most of the time.

"However, the organizations that did well were usually those who successfully decoded the local culture and needs: what the customers want, how to provide it to them, how to solve their problems and how to handle the various local challenges. These organizations were also wise enough to define long-term business objectives and a global strategy based on local human infrastructures – building a chain of talented local executives and employees.

"In nowadays reality, the successful organizations are those who adopt a global mindset, realizing that their role is not only to bring their own skills to the developing countries but also to merge, understand and share. These are the organizations that are able to internalize and incorporate the values of the new place to the same extent as the values they bring about as a foreign culture. Think about this aspect of integrating an existing business in a foreign culture, the aspiration for mutuality. You'll realize that it's impossible to underestimate the importance of skills such as empathy, flexibility and reality testing for executives in these places."

"And still," I said, "with due respect to empathy, you and I both know that eventually we are measured by the stockholders according to the quarterly results. Eventually, any long-term investment decreases short-term profits."

3. Sustainability

"You should note that this paradigm is no longer true. The bottom line of the profit and loss statement is no longer how the organizational results are presented to the stockholders. Another factor comes into play: **sustainability**, meaning the sustainability of the business, its ability to persist and maintain at least at the same level of success over time.

"More and more organizations realize that sustainability doesn't depend solely on short-term profit, but also on their public image. They also understand the long-term effect of their public image. The concept of success has widened and includes now a positive contribution to society as a whole, which means returning some of the profits and devoting some of the organizational activities to the community, the economy and the environment.

"Basically, what happened is that the sustainability of the business has become tightly linked to its contribution to the overall viability of the communities, the economies and the environments in which it operates.

"Executives in the 21st century must take into account this broader definition of success, use it when initiating a decision-making process and building a strategy, incorporate it in measurements and evaluation processes and explain it clearly to their stockholders."

Of all the things I had heard so far, this was the weirdest. "Now listen here, Rona. With all due respect to the environment and the community, today's businesses suffer from harsh competition. As they struggle to lower their expenses, you're talking about more spending. Eventually, no one will remember your generosity when your business collapses. After all, we do pay state taxes, property taxes and social security, and it's the state's job to help others, isn't it?"

"Michael, our entire society is changing and is empowered like never before. The current situation makes it impossible to ignore the issue of sustainability. In this respect, I believe we have better years ahead – when organizations won't be all about profits and will contribute to society as well. I know that PepsiCo, Cisco and IBM are already there. A highly esteemed Harvard professor, Rosabeth Moss Kanter, spearheads this type of process in leading global organizations. She published an excellent book in which she describes the contribution of these organizations to society.[4] She argues that organizations that are wise enough to work this way will continue to grow and profit."

"So you argue that processes foreseen by actuaries of risk, economists and others should make us completely change concepts which have evolved and proven themselves for more than a century? Where were these wise men before the last crisis? I believe that a significant part of what they're saying reflects the pressure which results from a decade of recession. But other than forecasts, do you have examples of evident changes?"

4. Technology

"Of course, and this leads me to one of the central factors in the creation of white water: **technology**. The internet world is constantly reinventing itself. Each time it takes over another aspect of our lives, work or leisure. Although I will focus on the internet and mostly on what is called Web 3.0, you should remember that, as we speak, my knowledge of recent technological trends may already be out-of-date.

"The first internet wave was based on static sites, intended just for public image and web presence, sites which merely promote the business but do not really offer to sell anything. Then, it surprised the business community with the rise of global sales sites such as Amazon, which also led to changes in consumption habits and to new business models.

"The second wave, Web 2.0, turned surfers into content producers. The rise of the social networks completely changed business models in the sectors of media, entertainment and advertising. This wave also permanently changed commerce, the banking system, etc.

"The third wave, Web 3.0, is mostly based on the high availability of technologies that are the backbone of what is now called "the cloud" – fast communication infrastructures, especially wireless, and the establishment of huge server farms, storing vast amounts of data and providing modular and flexible computing systems.

"I mentioned earlier the migration of services to rising economy countries. It is mainly the result of the availability of new information technologies: virtualization technologies which enable you to work with a person at the other end of the world as if he were in the next room. But that's just the tip of the iceberg…

"Consumers now enjoy a huge variety of devices and interfaces, mobile touchscreen devices which offer a total and even addictive experience. Overall, this is a revolution that not only changed the way we live and communicate, but also changed business models, human resources requirements, and what is required of us, the executives."

"Often, the internet is referred to as a 'disruptive technology,' because every wave of change disrupts business models and can topple giants who weren't prepared for it. At the same time, small unknown companies became large corporations such as Amazon, Google and Facebook. As consumers began flowing to the commerce sites, the media channels also relocated to the internet. Social networks feasted on the remains of people's attention and free time, taking what used to be the business of the old entertainment and marketing channels.

"As a business, if you don't join the new virtual worlds, you are left behind, unknown and unheard of. You simply don't exist anymore. As an individual, whether you are an executive or not, if you desire to progress professionally you must understand how these new technologies affect your profession. Otherwise, you belong to the past and linger there.

"But the influence of technology goes far beyond the business world. To understand the extent of technology's influence on the world, we only have to look at what happened in the Arab countries following the use of social media, mainly Facebook, YouTube and Twitter. Nowadays, it's impossible to hide anything in places where there is a cellular network, through which photographs and clips of individuals go directly online. The amazing technological developments of recent years have created a situation in which anyone with a cellular phone or a simple tablet can send reports to media networks. People can organize in social networks and use instant messaging systems to instantly organize masses of protesters either against a government or a business, that are perceived as harmful, exploiting or antisocial.

"Here, as it is throughout the Western world, governments and large organizations are under constant pressure on behalf of the public, which empowers social protest movement through the social media. It became very easy to boycott any certain brand. For the organization, this is no longer white water; it is a tsunami…"

"OK," I said, "you're talking about national or regional events. This goes beyond the influence or prediction abilities of a single organization, and certainly beyond that of a single executive or employee…"

"In a way, you're right. In comparison with the previous waves, the third internet wave is the least understood, even by CEOs. Even if most of them are aware of the great impact of technology on the organizations they lead, about 60% of them admit that they don't have a sufficient understanding of technology and its impact. You are surely unaware of that, but with the appearance of the internet, most CEOs dismissed it, thinking that it was some geeks' stuff, with no real business value. Do you get it?

"Today the situation is different; nobody can dismiss the technological changes and their consequences. I have recently talked to a senior executive who heads the IT department at one of the major banks. I realized that the lack of knowledge about what the future holds, from a technological standpoint, is driving everyone off balance.

"Everyone understands now that effectively handling the third internet wave is the biggest challenge of the next few decades. The popular concept is that the new technologies will create a larger revolution and will change business models in a way that will make Web 2.0 look like child's play."

"OK," I said, "I understand that technological progress requires adaptation and adjustment. But this change is eventually for the best! There are great opportunities here and, as an engineer, I personally find it very exciting. So, what's the problem?"

"This is no problem *per se*," she replied. "But, this definitely does require adaptation, flexibility and the ability to make optimal use of the new technologies to manage your work. But many organizations will find it difficult to cope with the change, as will some senior engineers. Don't take it personally…" The last comment came with a smile and a joking face. She also had a sense of humor…

5. Regulation

After a short pause, Rona continued her lecture. "This brings us to yet another change factor, **regulation**. Regardless of the organization I'm lecturing at – whenever I meet executives and talk about their challenges I know that the regulator is breathing down their necks. No matter the sector they operate in, regulation is increasingly dominant; restricting the organizations and their ability to operate freely. Executives know they must meet all the regulatory terms and develop stringent organizational discipline to comply with the requirements.

"It can be said that regulatory changes are a derivative of the magnitude and complexity of the changes we are witnessing in economy, technology and society. They are also an outcome of market failures that led to crises and protest movements. But regulatory changes lead and even force organizations to think differently; to think not only about the short-term or about immediate profit, but also about the longer term, in wider circles."

6. Generation Y

"Fine," I replied, "so how do we actually deal with all these changes? Let me guess, the answer is related to human resources?"

"True," Rona answered, "from the aspect of Human Resource Management we witness a significant change with the entrance of **the Generation Y**, another generator of white waters."

"Yes, I'm familiar with this generation," I immediately offered my personal experience, "I'm surrounded by them at work. Young and vibrant people who already know everything and expect to quickly get everything they want, soon after starting a new job – quick promotion, professional development, feedback at the press of a button, high salaries and much more…"

"True, Michael, there's no doubt that this generation is different from the former ones, the baby boomers and Generation X. This generation challenges managers and senior executives to an unprecedented degree. But more and more CEOs also realize that their ability to compete in global and local markets lies mainly in the quality of their employees: good employees mean good business performance and vice versa…

"In the past, many CEOs used to say 'people are our greatest asset,' but they didn't actually realize it. Now, actualizing this saying is critical for the growth of any organization. And so, it turns out that Human Resource Management has become a real war for talent – identifying and distinguishing the best from the less talented others, finding and attracting them and keeping them in the organization…"

"There," I rejoiced, "you say so yourself. The best should be kept and rewarded! We are returning to the old technical abilities: employees who are wizards in their area of expertise, brilliant and incisive."

7. Competition for Each Customer

"That isn't all!" Rona quickly curbed my enthusiasm. "But let's move on to the final factor that creates the white water. It is certainly last but not least, by order of importance: a **fierce competition for each customer**, whether this is an existing customer or a potential one.

"Customers and clients today are very picky: they demand higher quality services and products for half the price. On the other hand, much of those services and products have become commodities, which most companies can provide at about the same level of quality and price.

"In such a situation, all types of customers and clients, even CEOs and CFOs, are aware of their many choices. For this reason, each business organization feels it has to be more creative, reinvent itself and build a value proposition that is attractive and unique. Under such circumstances, the ability of executives and employees to connect and create a relationship based on trust, is critical. I'm talking about being able to become a 'trusted advisor' of one's strategic customers and not just a service vendor. You know, organizations can differentiate themselves in many ways. But in all aspects of communication with customers, the interpersonal skills of those who are in direct contact with the customers play a vital role."

The Consequences of the Change

"OK, so what does it all say about the management world and about me, as a manager, in the future?" I asked.

"As a manager, it is important for you to understand that continuous changes will keep on being a defining characteristic of the business and organizational environment. In order to thrive in such an environment, executives must be open-minded and know how to lead changes. Yesterday's reality doesn't exist today, and most certainly won't exist tomorrow. Executives must know how to handle the changes themselves – how to stay on the raft rather than falling into the white waters.

"Executives also need to know how to motivate and lead their employees through these times that are far more challenging and complex than ever before. Once, employees were mostly motivated using *'the carrot and the stick'* method. However, today their motivation requires much more. Daniel Pink emphasizes[5] that an executive must have high-level leadership skills, provide his employees with a sense of autonomy, enable them to become experts and grant them meaning in their work environment."

All of these will be discussed throughout our journey. I've picked a track for us, in order to focus and experience all the things we have talked about so far."

"I'm intrigued…"

"Very well… And if so, I would like to share some more insights with you and elaborate a little bit more on some of the white water generators that we've just introduced.

"The first and most significant one is that there will be, in the not-so-distant future, a heavy shortage of talented executives and employees, capable of managing and working in such a complex world of continuous and accelerating changes. Undoubtedly, in view of its uncertainty, this complex world requires broader skills and abilities for executives. Most people find it hard to change, so they cling to the mental maps that led them to success. Recently, the Center for Creative Leadership[6] conducted an interesting study. The study concluded that most organizations wouldn't appoint about 40% of their managers if they had to make the decision again."

This harsh and rather troubling statement is hard to accept, I thought to myself.

"I can see the wheels turning in your mind... Listen, I take part in many processes at some of the leading organizations here. I participate in meetings where they look for promotion candidates, and I can see how hard it is for managers to find suitable ones. For instance, Nathan has superb professional abilities but is incapable of managing a single employee; Emma has excellent leadership skills but isn't professional enough; Dana has good professional skills and her employees love her, but she is incapable of reaching the managements of her clients.

"One more thing you should know is that the most important skills for success are the soft ones, such as emotional intelligence. There are many people with a bachelor's, master's, or a doctoral degree. Generation Y loves to study. The economic situation drives them to spend more time in school and get one more degree, in order to improve their chances of being hired for one of the best positions.

"But the most important skills for success will ultimately be adaptability, interpersonal skills and emotional awareness. Think about your own work environment, and you will see that all those who succeeded in management positions, were those who also had high skills in these areas. One thing is certain: if emotional intelligence was important for success in the 20th century, it is critical for success in the 21st century. I see it as a consultant, and with executives undergoing various processes at their organizations.

"There is another aspect making emotional intelligence so important to the organization. Employees and executives will require extremely high emotional intelligence in order to retain existing customers and recruit new ones. Moreover, even the strongest and well-positioned organizations will need such people who possess the ability to build significant relationships with their customers, based on high trust levels and providing a real value proposition. Only when most of their executives have such abilities, can a management claim to be on the right path...

"And one more point: knowledge-expert employees will continue to control the market, and lifelong study will be a business requirement. This reminds me of some very interesting data I had come across in the *Harvard Business Review*. Twenty-five years ago, when a student graduated and joined the workforce, how much of the knowledge he had acquired during his studies would he use, in your opinion?"

"I would guess that most of it...?"

"Correct, the answer is about 75%. The rest of the knowledge was gradually acquired from professional guidebooks and individuals within the organization. After a certain amount of time, the knowledge he had acquired made him a professional. Dedication and experience made him an expert.

"Today, things are dramatically different: a typical graduate on his first job will use about 10% of the knowledge he acquired during his studies. This knowledge is not necessarily the most essential, or the most required for success on the job. Actually, his studies provided him with mostly a theoretical base of knowledge for his profession. From this point, through various positions he will hold, begins the acquisition of practical knowledge and experience in the real world.

"In an era of continuous innovation, the subject matter is not updated quickly enough, and a professional will have to acquire most of the required knowledge throughout his career. This need will probably never cease; both he and his more senior colleagues will have to continue to gain new knowledge, adapt to new technologies and to a changing reality. As a result, continual learning will be a business requirement. The expert of today cannot lie back, relax and believe that he's seen it all and knows it all.

"And more importantly, from my experience, I know that only those who truly love what they do, are capable of learning so much. If you don't love what you do, any learning process, whether individually or in a group, will be an unwelcome task, something you will try to avoid.

"As to the issue of generations, it is the first time in history that organizations employ individuals from four different generations in an environment where they must work together. These generations have different work ethics, expectations and values. One might also say that they speak different languages. Sometimes it appears to me as if they are people from different planets… The generation gap will influence any process in the organization: recruitment, promotion, benefits, career paths and the business itself, of course.

"But the generation which will dominate the market will definitely be Generation Y. This is a very challenging generation. It is the first generation growing up under what we call conscious parenting. Their parents talked to them and listened to them, telling them, 'if you dislike something, you don't have to do it' or 'it is important to me that you're happy and capable of success.'

"As a result, confident in their skills and talent, and despite the financial crisis, they arrive at the workplace with high ambitions and expectations. They want to have it all, as soon as possible: fast promotion, high salary, work-life balance, an executive talk after one single week on the job... Also, if the job or the workplace doesn't please them, they are quick to leave for a better place. I discovered that some of them don't even resign – they are unaware of the existence of such a process at organizations..."

"Yes," I laughed, "I've already told you that I work with some of these kids. They live with their parents, drive their parents' cars and spend their parents' money... This is a generation of people that are capable of quitting a job after a single quarter, being ready to move on to the next thing. I must admit that from what I have seen, the greatest problem of this generation is that their self-esteem is in inverse proportion to their experience."

"True, but don't be confused, Michael. This generation will make the world a better place for all of us. And do you know why? Because this is the first time in organizational history that organizations are changing their strategies in order to retain their best employees. A significant percentage of organizations understand that people is all they really have. Such organizations, including the one in which you work, adapt an *'Employer of Choice'* strategy as the answer to the question of what they should do, in order to become the first choice of the best employees, to succeed in retaining them over time, and most importantly – to keep and promote the most suitable ones to management and leadership positions."

"And your job is to find the best," I added.

"Of course it is. The up-to-date Human Resources Department plays a central and crucial role, as any successful organization will obtain growth from such a progressive HR department that is aligned with the organizational strategy, providing significant added value.

"Now, it is also important to know that executives who succeed in the 21st century are those who integrate high professional abilities, high emotional intelligence and strong business skills. They are those who understand their business and the business of their customers. It is the HR department's duty to find such candidates for executive positions or to promote these skills among existing executives."

"So how do we actually get there?"

"There is no doubt that in your case, we'll have to go through the whole five lands journey mentioned by Martha, and get to know those lands closely. Like every journey, you can obtain exciting and meaningful experiences from each place. Like every journey, this one will also introduce you to new sights, cultures and people. And like every journey, you will have to cope with new experiences in terms of uncertainty, meet challenges and correctly allocate your resources.

"But after all, in this journey, the emphasis is on an internal, mental and emotional change that you will have to undergo. Do not panic… I'm not talking about a spiritual experience. I'm talking about acquiring skills – most of which are measurable; you'll be surprised to learn. These skills will enable you to act from a better place, from a position of leadership, power and awareness."

"So, when and where are we going?" I asked, surprised by the intensity of my enthusiasm.

"We're leaving early tomorrow morning. I know you don't have much time to pack, but we don't need much for such a journey. What we need most is an open mind. I'll meet you two hours before boarding; I have a few important messages for you before you set off."

That night, before leaving, I gave up on trying to sleep. As I packed a small suitcase, I was unable to part with the skepticism that accompanied me in spite of my great excitement and curiosity. I tried to rearrange my thoughts and cope with the fears that rose, hoping that this journey would not become a worthless experience that would hinder me in one of my most significant projects.

When I met Rona at the coffee counter, at the airport, she appeared fresh, though slightly pensive. "Hello Michael," she said and smiled her wide smile, "I'm happy to see you. I know it wasn't easy for you to take the first step and go on the journey. Let's get a table and see what's happening here before we board the plane."

Did we come to look at people? – I thought to myself. Is this why she asked me to come early to the airport?

"I know it sounds trivial, Michael, but one of the most important things to remember is that each of us is unique – a world in itself. Do you see the couple seated next to us, hardly talking? Did you notice the father explaining to his daughter why she can't have the expensive doll? Look at the woman sitting and smoking one cigarette after another and the businessman who can't stop talking on his cell phone and working on his computer. Do you see that beautiful cashier that everyone is checking out? Each of them has in his mind its own mental map, or if you wish, its own thinking pattern or mindset. Our actions, our decisions and our considerations, the extent of the effort we make, and our faith in ourselves – these are all the consequences of mindsets."

"And what does it all have to do with management?" I asked.

"As an executive, it is important for you to become acquainted with two major types of thinking patterns: the fixed mindset and the growth mindset.[7] Understanding these two thinking patterns and telling them apart is one of the most important lessons, and without them it is impossible to move on. Soon we will see how these concepts influence our daily lives – both our organizational and personal lives. You don't have children yet, but later on you will find out that your understanding of these two concepts will significantly influence your children and their lives."

At this point, once again, I felt as if I had made a mistake by setting out on this journey. What was she talking about? What did my promotion at work have to do with the children I didn't have yet? As I tried to quiet the critical voice inside, I heard the call: "Passengers on Flight 311 to Mindset Land, please report to gate No. 4."

"But Rona!" I yelled, trying to make myself heard over the loud noise from the jet's engines during takeoff, "At the end of the journey, how will I know if I've succeeded?"

Rona smiled and replied "You will know it once you can't keep all the insights you have acquired to yourself; when you have a tremendous urge to share with the rest of the world; when you come back to work and strive for all your nearest and dearest to internalize these insights; when you don't understand how it is possible to think or act otherwise. Then you'll know you have successfully taken the journey and have become a leader fit for the 21st century."

2
Mindset Land

The destination Rona chose to begin with was called Mindset Land. She explained that the term mindset means a thinking pattern.

We arrived early in the morning. As the pilot descended for landing, Rona drew my attention to a long river, stretching from the horizon to the ocean. On one of the river's banks, was a colorful and upbeat urban area, while there were straight lines of dreary and gray buildings on the other bank. Rona told me these were the two banks of the capital city of Mindset Land. I was hoping to start our tour from the colorful side of the city, which seemed much more interesting and appealing.

The landing was soft. From the airport, we drove to town and started sightseeing around the streets. We walked a lot and talked little. I guess that Rona wanted me to experience the place on my own and have an unbiased impression of it.

Well, my first impression of the place, as I saw it from the plane's window, turned out to be true. The urban scene on the west side of the city, where we started our tour, was indeed colorful, lively and exciting. Impressive buildings were everywhere, and the most prominent thing was the wide diversity of styles. We saw skyscrapers alongside ornate cathedrals, lively piazzas with sculptures and fountains and many entertainment centers: art galleries, theaters and cinemas. Advertising posters for dozens of shows were posted, and everywhere we looked there were street shows and open-air concerts. Plenty of museums were surrounded by gardens and parks. We saw a variety of stores and small boutiques that were adjacent to large shopping malls. The business sector made it clear that this city was a large commercial and economic center. On the modern buildings we saw signs with logos of Banks, Financial companies and technology companies such as Google, Microsoft and Facebook. In the broad spaces between the buildings, we saw people rushing to work with cups of coffee in their hands. But here, unlike other commercial cities I had visited around the world, I saw smiling people who seemed pleased and relaxed. It clearly appeared that they were enthusiastic and even passionate about their activities.

The interesting thing was that in each piazza, regardless of its size, was a colorful and creatively designed homage monuments, dedicated to men and women who "made it," decorated with portraits and description of their lives and accomplishments. These commentaries portrayed the concept that was the foundation of their achievements, the challenges they faced on their way, and praises for their determination and efforts. These monuments impressed me and added a facet of intimacy to the lively place. Even after three hours of touring,

I still felt that I would like to continue and spend more time in this city.

When we reached the main street, referred to by the locals as "the restaurants' street," we discovered a beautiful mall, paved in stone. It had all kinds of restaurants – Italian, Chinese, Japanese, Cuban, Portuguese, and many others. Astounded by the abundance and the sense of unlimited possibilities, I suggested having lunch.

We finally chose a local tapas bar, sat in its well-groomed yard and let the waiter take our order. I was surprised that immediately afterward, a kind and hearty man carrying a tray with plates of food approached us. He introduced himself as Mario, the owner. Mario was interested to find out where we came from and told us about his restaurant. After a while, I expressed my surprise that such a successful restaurant owner could find the time to talk to his customers at such a busy time of day. He laughed and said that his curiosity and desire to learn from new people were his guidelines, the same guidelines that served all the other citizens on this side of the river.

"The people on this side of the river are curious people. We are constantly learning new things, growing and evolving," he said, smiling.

When he saw my confused look, he further explained, "Unlike our neighbors on the other side of the river, we were nurtured by the understanding that regardless of our starting point, the most important thing in life is to continuously learn and develop. We believe that personal skills develop and intensify throughout life."

He continued to tell us that their lives were guided by the

concept that the brain itself is a flexible and dynamic organ, capable of changing and growing through learning and practice.

"Did you just say that the brain changes?" I wondered skeptically, "In what aspect? After all, it's well known that intelligence remains fixed from an early age and does not change."

"The brain certainly does change," Mario continued. "When we learn languages, arithmetic, music and sports, we train our brain. It's well known that the number of connections between the brain cells and their quality determines the complexity of the actions the brain is capable of performing. Training and stimulating the brain strengthens existing connections and even creates new ones. It is, therefore, possible to enhance one's abilities over time and improve its performance. As we cope with more challenges, our brain develops. This is why here, on the west side of Mindset Land, many individuals handle a wide variety of interests at the same time and are not afraid to dare and leave their comfort zones."

"So, does that mean that everyone here believes they can succeed in whatever they choose, if only they practice, work hard and apply themselves?" I asked.

"No, definitely not… We have a positive, yet realistic idea of our abilities and we're well aware of the fact that an individual can neither nor should expect to be equally good at all things. As far as we are concerned, success is our ability to act resolutely and invest our efforts in order to learn something new and develop. For this reason, failure is also a learning opportunity."

While listening to him, I wondered if he really meant what he said about failure. I have heard so many sentences such as "failure is an inseparable part of success" in my life. But, in fact, it is obvious to everyone that these sentences don't offer any comfort when you actually fail. However, Mario sounded very convinced to me…

"Excuse me for asking, Mario, but aren't you idealizing failure? According to you, it sounds like we should all aspire to fail – in order to learn and grow…"

"No, no one likes to fail," Mario answered, "but it seems to me that what you call failure, my friend, is not what I call failure. Your criterion for success or failure is the result, the bottom line. To us, the process is what counts, and 'failure' is to remain stagnant in one place – even if that place is a good and prestigious one. Failure is the unwillingness or inability to invest an effort in order to realize your potential. Failure is stagnation and the lack of persistence when facing challenges.

"Therefore, even if you did accomplish some goals, we wouldn't consider it a success if you did it through a wrong or fixed-minded process that wasn't accompanied by any development, effort or learning on your behalf. To us, success is the ability to meet challenges in order to expand our horizons and grow."

"If you tell me that for you, success is not measured by results, there's indeed a gap between our cultures," I said.

"Probably," Mario replied. "I don't know the country you come from. But if it's similar to other developed countries, I guess it's a society that worships quick and superficial performance and doesn't endorse gradual and profound processes.

"I'm very proud of the place where I grew up and the values I was raised on. From a young age, we were taught that through desire and effort, it is possible to nurture skills and personality, and to be more successful. We never received excessive praise for our personalities, since that kind of recognition produces dependency and adversely affects the willingness to strive and work hard for a goal or objective. What we did get as children, and passed on to ours, was the encouragement to work hard and make an effort. We believe that this is the key to a growth mindset and to realizing our potential."

"And how do you know when you've realized your full potential?"

"Maybe I will never know. But between you and me, what does it matter? It's obvious that it is impossible to predict where each of us will be years from now, neither is it important, as long as will, persistence and determination exist. We try a wide variety of things and dare to take chances, and this promotes us. Both children and adults are filled with passion for learning, development and challenges. They overcome their disadvantages rather than hide them. To us, life is a journey – every day we evolve and become stronger, more talented and more competent."

"But, don't you care if you are really talented in a certain area, an area on which you should totally focus?" I wondered, "After all, apart from your subjective experiences, there certainly is an objective reality. Or isn't there?"

"We can tell where we stand through our readiness to receive honest feedback from our environment. As we provide each other with constructive comments, we get to know our strengths and weaknesses. We are capable of evaluating our abilities, skills and performance. This knowledge serves us as a development tool. Of course, it also helps us to stay focused and realistic, and not overestimate ourselves.

"If you believe that you can grow and develop, that errors are an inseparable part of your way, and that the way to realize your potential is a journey rather than a destination – you will find it easy to accept the information provided by others, teachers and coaches, managers and colleagues, regarding your abilities."

Mario's speech inspired me to think and reconsider decisions I had made in the past. I also remembered events such as the one when I was insensitive to Tami, my team member, or the circumstances which led to my replacement in the project with the Germans.

As I tried to understand what had driven me to make such decisions, I realized that I often clung on to what I already knew. It seems that I only participated in projects where I knew I could express my strengths. When was the last time I actually left my comfort zone, daring to examine or explore something new without fear, even if it meant coping with my weaknesses? For a long time, I felt that my work and, to be honest, my personal life as well, were a collection of tests that required me to prove myself. Actually, I was probably considered to have failed by the standards of the Mindset Land.

"Michael, it's time to move on, we should get going to the other side of the city, the east side," I heard Rona's voice. She was silent, but attentively listening, during the entire conversation. "We'll cross the river by boat," she added. We said goodbye to Mario and proceeded to the pier on the river bank.

***

As we reached the river, I was astounded by the river's flow and width, the floating plants along the bank and the old water mill. We saw ditches with ancient wooden bridges and were surrounded by merry fishermen and bathers of all ages. Everything seemed so full of life, and yet so calm.

We hired a small boat to take us to the opposite bank, and throughout the entire cruise I thought about Mario's words – the most important things are the investment of effort, learning and development. What does that mean to me?

About 10 minutes later we were standing on the opposite river bank. The fishermen and bathers were here as well, but the atmosphere was less pleasant. We got off the boat and marched from the pier until we reached a main street paved in stone, with buildings that were surprisingly alike. We saw simple looking churches, entrances to subway stations and many industrial buildings. The streets were clean, but they lacked grace. The uniformity was also evident in the residential buildings and in the appearance of the people, who looked as if they were cast from a single mold. They all wore dark clothes and seemed troubled and self-centered. Their facial expressions were similar and monotonous. I looked at the billboards and saw posters advertising a single movie and a single show, a striking paucity compared to the richness and the cultural diversity on the other bank.

I walked around, feeling that we had gone from a dynamic and vivid place to a stagnant place that got stuck in the past. I asked Rona if we were in the older part of the city.

Rona smiled, "Actually, this side is newer. Surprising, isn't it? We're on our way to meet a local guide to get some background about the culture and the history of the locals. You can ask him anything."

After walking through drab streets, we reached a coffee shop where a tour guide by the name of Tom was waiting for us. The coffee shop belonged to a local chain, a kind of 'drink & go', very different from the intimate and pleasant coffee shops on the opposite bank. Rona, who sensed that I was uncomfortable, said, "Michael, you can ask Tom whatever crosses your mind about this place. This is why he's here."

Since Tom looked like a person who wasn't enthusiastic about his work and would gladly be doing something else, I politely asked him how many years he had been doing his job. He smiled at me and said, "Too many."

"Don't you enjoy your work?" I asked.

"Well, tour guiding was never my dream job," he answered.

"And what is your dream job, if I may ask?" I further asked him.

"Since I was a child, my great passion was animals," Tom said, and by the look on his face, I felt that he appreciated the interest I was taking in his life. "I always dreamed of becoming a veterinarian. But, in order to be accepted to a veterinary school here, one has to pass difficult exams. I never applied because the odds were that I would never pass them."

I was surprised by the ease with which he gave up his dream. "Why weren't you more persistent?" I asked. "And, even if you had failed, couldn't you retake the tests?"

"It's interesting you should ask this," He answered, "because a friend of mine, who has similar skills to mine, applied once and failed. Then he studied for the tests for an entire year and passed them the second time. Today, he's indeed a successful veterinarian."

"So, why couldn't you do what he did? What's the difference between the two of you?"

"The difference between us is that when he was a child, my friend moved with his parents to the west side of Mindset Land." Tom smiled ironically and explained, "You see, geographically, there is just a river between the two parts of this land, but mentally, there is an ocean between us. The west side is a place where you can always get a second chance."

"Please explain this," I asked.

"Here, on the east side of Mindset Land, we believe that all people are born with a certain amount of intelligence and talent which remains constant through life. When they're in elementary school, young children receive an evaluation from their teachers regarding their abilities – their talent and professional orientation. These assessments rely mainly on ability tests according to which the children and their parents will make their decisions. My teachers thought that I wasn't born with the skills to be a veterinarian because I never excelled in life science."

"But, what about effort and hard work?" Mario's speech came back to me. "Didn't your parents and teachers take these into account, as a means for success?"

"Here we believe that you either have it or you don't," Tom said with a bitter smile on his face. "If you don't, it is all lost for you. You won't be able to change the direction that your life is bound to take."

"This is the exact opposite of the concept of growth, in which they believe in the opposite side of the river," I noted.

"True, it is completely different. They also believe that innate talent is important, but it simply isn't the most important factor for success. They argue that each and every one of us has individual strengths and that one can develop and achieve almost anything with hard work, training and effort. The sky is the limit; that's their motto."

"So what is considered success around here?" I asked curiously.

"That's an interesting question, and the basis of everything. Here, success is measured by the result. If we demonstrate our abilities and talents in a noticeable and measurable way right from the beginning, we will be empowered by the environment."

"And do you have successful people who have made it, like on the other side?"

"We do, but very few of them. If you don't stand out with your extraordinary talent, you won't even try, because it's obvious you can't achieve like these few stars. Those who do succeed are at the top of their category. When they are at the peak of their success, you can easily recognize them. Whether athletes, musicians or businessmen – when they're at the top, they're sure that they are the closest thing to God. In view of their success, they act arrogantly and disrespectfully toward others.

"But the real sad thing is that their success doesn't last very long, in many cases. Once reality changes and they have to do things differently or to invest effort in new directions, something happens to them. They give up and start to decline."

"How do you explain their inability to adjust to reality?" I asked.

At this point, Rona stepped into the conversation. "By the sound of it, they expect everything around them to change back so that they can recreate their success. But they don't take the time to look at themselves – their own contribution to their decline and what they should do to recreate their success. After all, being so talented, they can't possibly be the problem…"

Tom nodded in assent and said, "There's another factor keeping the most successful ones from investing effort to maintain their success. Here, we worship extraordinary talents and abilities. Effort is perceived as contrary to natural talent: talent is innate, and it is yours for good. That's why it's believed that if you are truly talented you don't need to work hard and sweat.

"Failure takes those who have succeeded by surprise and exposes their weaknesses, which were mostly unknown, even to themselves. If you've been glorified by your environment throughout your entire life – a setback or temporary failure means that you are not so talented, after all. It means that you should make way for those who really are. From this point onward, two factors lead to a state of disability: fear of coping with another failure, and fear that people will see you're putting in effort and deduce that you're actually less talented than they thought.

"And this is the most difficult thing – to see all those fallen stars. It's one thing not to be successful from the start. But, to turn into a star, and then to have others figure out you aren't a prodigy – becomes a terrible fall to the individual and his family, one that can be remembered for long. This is why most of those stars will do everything they can, to prevent others from seeing that they sometimes slip up, experience difficulties or need to work hard. Here, on this side of Mindset Land, the fear of failure is much greater than the desire to succeed."

At this point, I couldn't restrain myself. I asked Tom how he explained the immense gap between the two parts of the land. "The conceptual difference between you and them is enormous and manifested in all areas of life – education, culture, construction, behavior and even external appearance. How is it possible? Where does it come from?"

Rona smiled and said, "To me, this is the key question. This is also the reason I chose to begin our journey here, in Mindset Land. Tom, I would like to tell Michael the story because it inspires and moves me time and time again."

Smiling, Tom nodded, and Rona continued.

"Mindset Land initially began on the other side of the river, the west side, where our tour began. The way they lived, as well as their beliefs and values, were very much as they are here today. They sanctified talent, believing that the innate, intrinsic competencies are fixed at birth and cannot be changed, thus labeling children according to anticipated fields of profession and interest, at a very young age.

"One day, a new teacher, Veronica, arrived at the leading school in town. They say that she came from another land. Veronica brought an innovative educational concept, which was contradictory to the common concept in Mindset Land. Veronica believed that valuing innate qualities alone and labeling the children according to them, narrowed their ability to succeed in life. She also believed that any individual had a variety of different competences, which continuously grew and evolved throughout life.

"Where she came from, she had wonderful professors. One of them was Howard Gardner, who developed the theory of multiple intelligences and expanded the traditional concept of intelligence, arguing that each and every one of us has a unique composition of three forms of intelligence.[8] Another of her teachers, Robert Sternberg, talked about successful intelligence, a combination of several components of intelligence.[9] According to this theory, one needs to combine and use the aspects of all those components.

"With such notions in mind, she came to the fixed educational system in Mindset Land. She found that the students were taught to think, talk and act alike. All students were required to learn the same subjects, and all were measured by the same tools.

"Since they believed that their skills were innate and fixed, children who were not considered 'smart' by the system were thought of as having limited ability. They were not invested in, and no one expected much of them. Children, whose parents and teachers didn't believe in their abilities, also stopped believing in themselves. They didn't work hard since they would never be able to change and become smarter. Veronica found it awful that the teachers and the parents didn't believe in their children's abilities. Their low grades were a ticket to a slow path of life.

"The high grades of the 'smart' students got them on the fast track to success. Ironically, they also felt that they didn't need to work hard – because they were talented, no matter what. And so, at a certain point, they stopped making progress.

"Veronica honestly believed that individuals could develop their skills through effort and hard work. In fact, she started the revolution on her own: she decided to change the situation, contacted her former professors, and constructed a unique curriculum with them.

"She instilled in her students the awareness that intelligence appeared in a variety of ways and expressions, and that talent alone wasn't enough to succeed. Constant work and practice were necessary. She showed them that some children were better in sports, others were talented musicians, and still others were better in logic, language, spatial orientation or social skills. She taught them that each and every one of them had different abilities that could be developed.

"Above all, she argued that your real challenge was to find your own talents, work hard and not give up, even when you encounter an obstacle. In her pleasant way, Veronica convinced the children that it was possible to view obstacles as gifts that assist us to develop and improve, and that these hardships and challenges teach us much more than constant success. In view of all this, you can imagine the reaction of the parents of those children as they understood the content that was being taught at school."

"I bet they were pleased. The rationale seems so correct," I said.

"A small group of parents did understand the rare opportunity these children were given, and supported the new spirit that Veronica introduced at school. But there was a strong opposition to her method from a larger group of parents. Veronica's name became prominent, and she was the hot subject in people's conversations for a long time, a subject of admiration or objection – depending on whom you asked."

"I can't understand the objections of these parents. After all, as she promoted their children, they must have seen the results."

"True," said Tom, who joined back into the conversation. "The students benefited from her, big time. And surprisingly, not just the 'weaker' children, but also the 'smarter' ones. Although, they were getting high grades, many of them were actually afraid and even anxious due to the high expectations from them.

"Despite the criticism, Veronica wouldn't give up. For instance, during the first few months she refused to submit the children to the school's Growth and Effectiveness Measures – so that they wouldn't be prematurely labeled. She also believed in opening diverse learning channels, and occupied the children with physical activity, singing and group dynamics.

"Many parents considered this a waste of precious time. There was a serious debate among the parents, and the argument heated up. Those who opposed her demanded to go back to the methods used thus far. They argued that Veronica's activity would impair the children's achievements and cause the school's level to drop. Those who supported her felt persecuted. However, since the school principal was supportive of her, a large group left angrily and started a settlement on the east side of the river. Since then, the people have been divided into two distinct groups, with an almost complete separation between the two sides."

***

I thought of Veronica, a single teacher with a mission, who was able to inspire so many individuals and change their reality. It reminded me of Jane, my eighth-grade teacher, who actually changed my life. She was the first one to believe in me, to look at me and see something beyond what everybody else saw. She became my homeroom teacher two years after I immigrated to Israel from Argentina with my family. By that time, I already had a reputation at school as a silent and introverted boy. At that point, the teachers had given up and didn't try to call on me, after two years of unsuccessful attempts to make me participate in class. I had no problem understanding them, but I was afraid the children would make fun of my accent. Besides, I was secretly hoping that if my parents saw that I wasn't adjusting, they would do an about-face. I wished we would all return to Argentina and I would be reunited with the friends I left behind.

Jane identified my abilities and made me feel she believed in me. She taught me to have faith in myself, to progress and grow. But now, in retrospect, despite all the progress I had made, I think that my success was only measured by grades. I never realized that just as investing an effort improves success in school; it might also bring about the same consequences in other areas of life such as relationships, business dealings, or coping with changes. In these areas, I had always thought exactly like the fixed-minded individuals here – you either have it or you don't. I remembered many conversations with John and his attempts to show me that, with effort, it was possible to develop interpersonal skills. These efforts on his part passed me by, unnoticed.

***

"How about we go back to the west side of the city, where we started our visit? We'll stroll around the piazzas. There are some more people I would like to tell you about. Some of them you might not recognize, but you will recognize some as famous and successful."

I was thrilled by the invitation to leave the gloomy atmosphere behind and go back to the nicer and more interesting side of the city. We thanked Tom and sailed back to the other bank. Rona showed me an old picture of a child and asked, "Do you recognize this tall boy holding the basketball?"

"Not really…"

"His name is Michael Jordan. Does that ring a bell?"

"Sure, I know him as an adult player, but I didn't recognize him as a child."

"What do you think of him?"

"I think he's the best basketball player of all times, he's an innate phenomenal talent, and you won't find another player to match his abilities today."

"I agree with the second part of your observation, there's no player to match him today. However, I disagree about the role of his phenomenal talent in his success. Clearly, he was born with great talent, but this isn't the entire story. I want to share some stories that might be new to you. Did you know that he was cut from his high school team, when he was 15? His coach argued that he wasn't fit to be a team player and assigned him to the junior varsity team."

"This is hard to believe," I was surprised.

"Also, he didn't make the cut the first time he tried to join the basketball team at the University of North Carolina. As a result, he didn't meet the professional standard required by scholarship applicants. And, believe it or not, before he became a superstar, he didn't make the cut on two NBA teams."

"Are you sure?"

"Definitely. And do you know what his mother said to him when the coach cut him off the team? She said he wasn't disciplined enough and didn't practice sufficiently. She said that if he took himself seriously and practiced he would improve and become a master. So, he took her advice seriously and started practicing with determination – getting up at five o'clock every morning and practicing as hard as he could. In fact, in all the years he played basketball he never stopped practicing. He became the most devoted NBA player, who practiced even after games, whether his team won or lost. The assistant coach of the Chicago Bulls once said that he is a genius constantly perfecting his genius quality. When asked how he did it, Michael Jordan simply answered, 'I just keep throwing the ball.'"

"And he who throws more, scores more. This is obvious," I said.

"Are you familiar with the 10,000 hours rule?"

"No…"

"This is a rule formulated by the Canadian writer Malcolm Gladwell, in his book *Outliers*.[10] This rule states that in order to achieve mastery in a field, you must practice for about 10,000 hours – which may take 5 to 10 years. When we see an extraordinary athlete, a Nobel Prize laureate or a fabulous musician, we do not see what happens backstage. We don't see the many hours of effort they put in, the sweat and the disappointments they had experienced to achieve their greatest achievements. We think that such people are simply geniuses or lucky. But it is obvious that high-level personal ability and even genius quality are not a guarantee of success. They are most certainly a good thing to start with, but it's impossible to reach extraordinary achievements without hard work and without risking failure. As Michael Jordan said, when asked what was the secret of his success – 'I failed over and over in my life and that is why I succeed.'"

"I have another example of the importance of hard work on the road to success," Rona said. "At the music academy in Berlin, teachers were asked to divide their violinist students into three groups. The first was the group of elite performers, students who had a high potential of becoming world-renowned musicians. The second group included those who were considered 'good' or professional. In the third group were the less able performers that were actually designated to become music teachers. All the students were asked an identical question: 'How much time did you practice throughout your career since you first held the violin?'"

"It turned out that during the initial stages of study, when they were about five years old and started to play, they all practiced for about the same number of hours. But as the years went by, substantial gaps were created. And so, by the time they were 20 years old, the 'stars' had accumulated about ten thousand hours of practice, while the 'good' violinists about eight thousand. The future music teachers had only four thousand hours of practice.

"You see, it doesn't matter what the occupation in question is – sports, chess, ice skating, science or teaching… Those who reached the top are those who have invested many hours and worked much harder than anyone else."

"If the crucial role of investment and determination is so well known, how come the inhabitants of the gloomy, eastern side of this land don't adopt this attitude?" I asked.

"As the years go by, there is a slow immigration of people to the western side. But many still stay on the fixed minded eastern side and are either not interested or incapable of opening up to new perceptions. It's possible that they are afraid to make the effort and leave their comfort zone. These people are deeply set in their fixation, but you and I can still make a choice.

"You have a choice, Michael. You can choose which bank of the river you want to live on: whether to stay fixated about your abilities and skills or to adopt a growth mindset. By choosing a growth mindset you choose a path by which hard work and effort will bring about achievements in all areas, even in those in which you are currently less capable."

She is right, I thought to myself. It was up to me – whether to keep dragging in my comfort zone, retaining what I had, without taking any risks, or to open up to challenges and risks as opportunities to progress and grow.

"Say, Rona, how is it that so many managers aren't too familiar with these terms? And why isn't anyone addressing such an important and dominant issue?"

"Some people deal with mindsets, and the most prominent of them is a highly distinguished professor from Stanford University, Carol Dweck. I told you about her just before we boarded the plane. She's been dealing with this issue for more than 20 years."

"Why haven't I heard of her?"

"Her work gradually becomes more widely recognized. Her groundbreaking book on Mindset[11] generated considerable interest from readers, and is highly important to me. In this book, you can learn a lot about mindsets and their influence on a variety of aspects of our life. This book will undoubtedly convince you that our mindset deeply influences our professional and personal achievements, differentiating those who achieve their goals from those who don't."

"I'll add it to my reading list," I said with a smile.

"Michael, do you know why the mindset is so critical, especially in the 21st century? That's because, as I told you, reality is constantly changing. For this reason, the existing repertoire that led us to success at a certain stage, is insufficient in the next phase. As a result of this changing reality, the concept of leadership also undergoes a significant change. We will see more and more leaders who develop their skills through learning, throughout life; because this pattern of growth will lead to progress and success. Or, as John Kotter from Harvard argued in his book, *Leading Change*[12] – changing the behavior of individuals is the most important challenge for business organizations attempting to compete in a world dominated by changes and crises."

"Before we move on, I would like you to look at your tablet and see the summary I sent you."

In the changing world of today, the successful managers will be the ones who...

- Understand that as managers, they have to change.
- Adopt a growth mindset.
- Understand that practice, learning and development are a part of their work.
- Evaluate their performance and their skills effectively and work hard in order to develop.
- Internalize that change entails a certain amount of risk, but risk management is anyway part of their job as managers.
- Realize that change includes learning: if you do not learn, you will become irrelevant.
- Remember that change must come with effort: if you do not put in sufficient effort, you won't be a part of the game.

We continued touring the lively streets, and in my head, I heard myself repeating the mantra "people do not change" in various conversations with John and Martha. I felt a wave of embarrassment and shame. I understood why Rona said that our first destination was of crucial importance in our journey and that no significant process could take place without it. I consciously decided to try to adopt the attitude of the river bank I first arrived at and to remind myself that determination, hard work, experiment and practice were valuable skills for success.

Looking forward to know what our next destination is, I heard Rona saying, "Michael, we must go now to the airport. Our flight leaves in two hours." At the airport's gate, Rona told me that our next destination was a fascinating land, a kingdom led by *King M the Fourth*.

Needless to say, his name sounded quite peculiar to me…

3
Whole Brain Land

The landing was smooth. The plane touched down, and I didn't even feel the queasiness that I often experience during landings.

As we left the airport, I saw the strangest and most surreal sight I have ever seen. All the people on the street had their heads tilted! They were walking, talking, drinking coffee and reading the newspaper with their heads tilted at quite a sharp angle. This fascinating and bizarre sight is hard to describe, you just have to see it to believe it! The only normal-looking individuals were the children, who had only a slight tilt of the head or none at all.

"What's going on here?" I asked Rona, "An entire land of people with tilted heads? What is it? Is it a genetic neck problem in a whole population?"

"Not at all, Michael, this is not a genetic flaw, but a physical expression of a brain preference. Now, take a good look at the people to see the nuances. Notice that some of the heads are tilted to the right while others to the left. Some display only a slight angle while others display a sharper one."

Truth be told, I had noticed these differences, but I didn't give it much thought. So, what was this brain preference that Rona spoke about? And why was it so noticeably expressed in the physical stature of these people? How come a slight tilt in childhood became sharper as they grew up? And finally, why were some of the heads tilted at a sharper angle than others?

All of these questions preoccupied me. "Do you think we appear strange to the locals, just as they appear strange to us?" I asked. Rona smiled and nodded.

"So, what's the difference between people with a right-hand or a left-hand tilt?" I yelled to make myself heard over the noisy crowd that surrounded us.

Rona gestured that she couldn't hear me, because of the tumult in the streets. Children and adults were walking in the streets, and the atmosphere seemed festive. The coffee shops and restaurants were flooded with diners. It looked as if everyone was having a good time and I wondered if they were celebrating a local tradition.

But I also sensed that it wasn't just the noise that kept Rona from answering me. She must have wanted me to take in the situation by myself. That is why I continued looking at the passersby, trying to figure out what was really happening in this strange land.

As we were walking in the streets, carried away by the masses, we heard there would be a ceremony in 15 minutes in the town square, by the king's palace. The very existence of a monarchy, in such a place that has a modern appearance, really surprised me. But I gave up the attempt to figure it out. Instead, I tried to focus and find a way through the masses hurrying toward the town square.

A great crowd was gathered in front of the palace, and giant plasma screens in the adjacent streets enabled the masses to see what was going on. Loud applause rang out everywhere as the announcer invited *King M the Fourth* to take the stage. The king, who looked as if he came out of an old fairytale book, opened the ceremony in a warm voice, filled with enthusiasm:

My beloved people! As you all know, our kingdom, which was once prosperous and successful, is currently in distress. We have tried our best to overcome the difficulties, but our attempts have failed in view of the frequent global crises and rising unemployment. At this point in time, it appears that the survival of our current practices and traditions does not stand much of a chance. Therefore, after days and nights of consulting with our best experts, I can do nothing but be as responsible as I can, and turn the kingdom over to new hands.

I can imagine your feelings upon hearing this news, and I admit that, personally, I too am filled with a fear of walking toward the unknown. But at such moments it is important to remember that we are not the first to deal with this kind of a situation and probably other lands will follow. My advisors have searched the books and found out that such dramatic events occur about once in two hundred years, and it is happening now. I call upon all of you to be united, to accept the difficulty as a challenge and to hope that the change will be for the best. We have reached the stage in which we must try to remember how to use the additional parts of the brain, the ones that each of us has neglected over the years. Therefore, I am turning the kingdom over to the Quadra Modals!

"He means those who make use of all four parts of the brain!" Rona explained as I was wondering – what was going on here? How come the brain had suddenly acquired two more parts, in the past hour since I first heard about the two parts of the brain?

The crowd in the streets was excited, and shouts of "Long live the King!" sounded everywhere.

"Let's go to the nearby university, we can talk there," Rona proposed.

We made our way through the crowd and reached the campus, where we sat at a coffee shop, enjoying relative peace and quiet. I sat back in my chair, took a sip of coffee and asked Rona, "What did the king mean when he said that certain parts of the brain were neglected? And what does all of this have to do with their success?"

Rona took her time before answering me. "Do you remember the lessons from the journey to Mindset Land?"

I nodded.

"What is the most significant insight that you have from there?"

"I understand now that people who will succeed in the 21st century will have a growth mindset which will enable them to adapt to the changing reality."

"True. This is indeed a necessary condition for success in the 21st century, but it's not a sufficient one. Because even those who do have a growth mindset still have to use all four parts of the brain in a harmonious manner, in order to succeed."

"And what are the four parts of the brain?" I asked.

"Soon, we'll hear a detailed explanation from a team of leading brain researchers, here at the university. But before meeting them, let's start from the basic model dividing the brain into two primary parts – left and right. According to this model, the left side of the brain is mostly responsible for precise activities such as logical thinking, language skills and identification of information. On the other hand, the right side of the brain is mostly used for abstractions, identifying nuances and fitting information into bigger schemes. Therefore, individuals with a so-called left-brain tendency are rational and analytic: they rely on facts, numbers and details – people who check the applied aspect of things. Those with a right-brain preference are intuitive, creative, verbal characters – people who look at the bigger picture."

"Is this division scientifically valid?" I wondered.

"Good question, and one that definitely reflects your brain tendency," Rona answered in an amused tone. "As you very well know, there is still much that we do not know about the brain. I have no doubt that if you ask neurobiologists, they'll have their reservations about the simplistic division of right-brain and left-brain. They will probably say that any complex cognitive behavior obliges us to use both parts of the brain. It is obvious that proper functioning is possible only when both parts of the brain act in cooperation.

"So, it appears to me that we should treat this division as if it were a metaphor for two types of thinking: the logical-linear way and the creative-intuitive way. Mostly, it is the way we prefer and nurture a particular kind of thinking. In this land, we can clearly see the bizarre physical expression of this division. If you look around, you will also see that individuals with a certain brain tendency prefer the company of those who are like them. They sit at the same places, share interests, tend to choose related occupations and, in most cases, they also choose partners with the same brain tendency.

"Marriage between individuals with opposite brain tendency is rare here. It is actually considered a form of mixed marriage. Even though children of such parents are known to be multi-disciplinary and extremely talented, they find it difficult to adapt socially, and this is the reason such cases rarely occur. It appears that everyone wants to retain the familiar. They eventually educate their children according to the priorities and values which derive from their own brain tendency. Consequently, they search for a similar spouse. Parental investment in acquiring life skills characterized by their own brain tendency is dominant and thus, gradually, children resemble their parents."

"Fine," I said, "this explains why the head tilt of children is smaller and increases with age. But how do these two very different camps get along here, when the division is this clear?"

"As you have heard from the king, his kingdom knew many years of prosperity. But who do you think were the people who held the leading and senior positions? And who do you think are those who enjoyed the highest incomes?"

"If this is anything like our world, those people are probably the ones who developed the left part of their brain."

"True. During the past hundred years, there was a clear

hierarchic structure. The ones at the top of the pyramid were those who were inclined to use the left part of their brain. Engineers, accountants, economists, lawyers and bankers held pure knowledge in their hands. They had an advantage where rational thinking was concerned. They were successful, placed at the head of the organizational ladder: they had high salaries, excellent working conditions, respect and prestige. Individuals with right-brain dominance were going into professions such as teaching, counseling, social work and art. Some of them were able to get promoted, but the senior positions were never open to them, and the hegemony of those with the left-brain tendency was retained over the years."

"And then, what changed?"

"The change is related to the global process I mentioned, the shift from the knowledge era to the conceptual era. In Whole Brain Land, the signs of change appeared earlier than in the rest of the world, as a result of the sharp divide that exists here between right-brain and left-brain people. There are almost no in-betweens. So, eventually, the management methods didn't endorse cooperation and collaboration. The work environment became less supportive and less inclusive. There was no creative development, due to the emphasis on functionality. People became frustrated and felt unappreciated, which resulted in a gradual productivity decline. This crisis was topped with the relocation of some of the factories to countries where production is cheaper. Add to it a global economic instability, and there you have it: a kingdom in crisis."

"And what did the people do to emerge from the crisis?" I asked.

"There were attempts to heal the economy through local resources. But these attempts failed, and the king decided to seek outside help. He sent his advisors to review the literature, and they found a theory of an American researcher called Ned Herrmann, the Whole Brain Model,[13] which seemed to have been developed specially for them. Ned Herrmann was a physicist and musician who worked as a department head at General Electric. He coped with issues that affect this kingdom and, by the way, are a source of concern for every executive: how to increase the productivity, motivation and creativity of his employees.

"The king's advisors wrote Herrmann a letter describing their crisis. The letter touched Herrmann, and he sent a student of his, Peter, to try to help them find their way out. Peter brought a vast amount of knowledge which he had received from his teacher and presented it to the experts of the Brain Sciences Faculty.

"First, Herrmann relied on thorough studies about the lateralization of brain functions: the different specialization related to the left and right hemispheres of the brain. Notice that just as most of us have a dominant hand, foot or eye, we also have a dominant brain hemisphere. Naturally, in a pair of organs, the preference of one organ over the other also means more frequent use of it, increasing its performance in expert tasks. Similarly, the brain hemisphere which is more frequently used from a young age, becomes dominant and strengthens throughout life."

"Fine," I interrupted, "I understand that according to his model it is possible to develop skills for all parts of the brain through practice, just like you develop your muscles. But you haven't told me **what** the four parts actually are."

"True, because I wanted you to hear about them from Peter himself. I will only say that, based on his studies, Herrmann has added one more dimension to the lateral model of the right-brain and left-brain. The additional division results from the different specializations of the cerebral cortex and the limbic system. In general, the cerebral cortex plays a key role in cognitive functions, while the limbic system supports functions such as emotions, behavior and long-term memories. Thus, Herrmann outlines a four quadrants model of the brain, each of which results in a different thinking style and, accordingly, different reasoning skills and different styles of interaction with others. Additionally, our use of these four thinking styles shapes our mindsets and our approach to solving diverse problems.

"Peter is nearby, in the Faculty of Brain Sciences. For years, he has been studying and teaching, and is considered a senior lecturer. Let's go to meet him and hear a more detailed explanation of the Whole Brain Model."

On our way to the faculty, as we passed several areas in the university, it was apparent that most people there had their heads tilted to the left. I asked Rona if this attribute and expression of thinking style had become a screening tool for certain faculties, much like the SAT. Rona answered that it wasn't so. "However, people did choose to apply to programs according to their brain preference because they would rather study something that suits them, a profession which they will be good at."

We went to the top floor of the building and met a large and heterogeneous crowd of students, attesting to the fact that the issue of brain preference occupied both camps. We knocked on the door and entered Peter's office. Peter was a large man in his fifties with long black hair. He gazed at me for a long time, smiling. "I look at you and remember the first time I came here. I assume this is the first time you've met individuals with tilted heads."

"Yes, the sight is both bizarre and fascinating," I answered.

"And the underlying brain mechanism is even more fascinating," Peter said. "I understand that your interest in the model of the four brain parts developed by my teacher brings you here, so come, let's have a seat."

After we sat down, I asked Peter whether he believed that brain preference, thinking style, and their bizarre physical expression in the form of a head tilt, were genetic or nurtured.

"I'll try to simplify it," Peter answered. "The brain tendency is a product of both nature and nurture. For years now, we are no longer concerned with the quantification of the influences of heredity versus environment. Today, we focus on the practical aspect, on the influence of the environment. Each child is born with a unique set of qualities and personality traits. Then, the child is exposed to a certain reality through his parents, his teachers and his environment. As to the head tilt we observe in Whole Brain Land, it seems that the head starts to display some inclination around the age of three or four, when the brain tendency is formed.

"In comparison, both you and I have a preferred brain tendency which influences our abilities and choices, our decision-making process, and our relationships with ourselves and our surroundings. Yet, it has never resulted in the physical expression which is so typical and evident in this land.

"Now, let's take a better look at the details of the Whole Brain model," Peter said. "I will spare you the theoretical background of the model. From my years of experience, I know that people get lost when faced with physiological explanations, which take us away from the point. The point is the following table, or model map, which presents four thinking types and represents four different characters."

As Peter dimmed the lights, I could see a table entitled *"Ned Herrmann's Four Brain Styles"* [14] displayed on the screen:

A. *Logical & Analytical* Asks "What?"	D. *Explorer & Experimental* Asks "Why?" or "What If?"
B. *Safe-Keeping & Organized* Asks "How?" & "When?"	C. *Feeling & Relational* Asks "Who?"

"Now, let's see how each of those four different characters would face a change, as executives or as project managers – what is their approach and what questions will they ask?

"Clearly, project manager A is more logical and analytical. Focusing on facts and the bottom-line, he prefers numbers and charts. Seeking a realistic and clear vision of the process, he is critical and methodological. He enjoys problem-solving, debates, hacking and making things work. Finally, he controls processes by measuring performance and achievements.

"Project manager B seeks order and sequential procedures. His approach to a change process is to organize it in terms of how and when. He focuses on getting the tasks done by carefully planning those tasks in advance. He might feel somewhat insecure during the change, since he prefers predictable circumstances in which he can rely on past experience and confirmed methods."

"Those are certainly the left-brain people," I said.

"Exactly," Peter replied. "Now let's find out what characterizes right-brain people."

"Well, as Rona told me earlier, I guess they will be more emotional and sensitive, intuitive and creative."

"Indeed," Peter continued, "project manager C prefers to engage in dialogue about the change. He will focus on the team members and their roles, their feelings and relationships. Since he loves to help and mentor others, he will communicate the change and provide support. During the process, he will act as a team player, easily expressing his feelings and allowing others to do so. When facing problems, he will follow instincts and view challenges as growth opportunities.

"Finally, rather than tightly controlling and planning the process in advance, project manager D prefers having multiple options, leaving room for intuition and improvisation. He prefers to focus on 'the big picture' and the vision of how things will eventually be. Being an explorer, he will ask questions such as 'why' and 'what if' and may easily break the rules and take risks.

"Now, try to think which character is dominant in you, Michael, or maybe it is a combination of two characters," Peter told me.

I thought about it for a minute. "I guess I am an A type... or maybe an AB," I said, "but I'm not sure, there are moments when I feel like a D..."

"That's very logical. Each of us has one or two dominant types. However, for most of us, the preferences aren't too rigid. Under certain circumstances, it is possible to expand them. This is the issue at hand – how to expand our skills and diversify our courses of action. Our research teams work day and night to build tools that enable individuals to develop all four parts of the brain."

"To what end? To improve the employees' productivity?" I asked.

"That's just a side benefit. Please note that our knowledge about our individual position on the model map is a real asset at the personal level. It gives us an awareness of our strengths and weaknesses. It enables us to emphasize the development of dormant skills, so that we'll be able to apply them when the time comes. Awareness of our mindsets allows us to maximize our personal skills through better communication with our surroundings and to obtain new tools for problem-solving and effective learning methods."

"But, why emphasize our weaknesses? Shouldn't we do the opposite? Isn't it better to focus on further development of our strengths for better performance?" I asked.

"If we only focus on our strengths, our weaknesses will never improve. Let me better answer you with an example. Let's say that you're a manager with a left-hand brain preference, as you suggested, type A or B or a combination of both. Say you have a group of 10 employees you have to lead through a complex project. Most likely, your thinking pattern will lead you to focus on the technical aspects of the project: data processing, applicability, paying attention to the small details. All these will be highly prioritized by you, and your communication with your employees will be limited to mere technicalities. In addition, you won't consider your employees' opinions valuable unless they are supported by facts. But this is exactly how you miss out from benefitting from those team members who have different skills, different thinking styles.

"Besides, surely you realize that an AB type manager doesn't indulge in questions such as 'How can I make my employees feel better?' He's always busy dictating the rhythm, concentrating on how to make their work more effective, more efficient. But some of his best employees, in order to connect with the mission and give it their best shot, need a sense of autonomy, expertise and meaning. This kind of manager hardly stands a chance at linking them to the project and getting their best. As a result, some of the employees become less efficient and may even be left out. Often, these are the best employees, the ones whom the organization would desire to retain."

"Moreover," Rona jumped in, "innovation is the most required skill in the 21st century. How can such a methodical and analytic manager who acts by the rules and avoids risks lead his employees to innovation?"

"Well said," Peter replied and continued, "Today, it's evident that organizations that do not reinvent themselves will disappear. In addition, most leading managers are AB types. The combination of these two factors has led our economy to the crisis which is being felt by so many.

"I'll give you another example to emphasize the importance of developing all four parts of the brain. Suppose you, as a manager, are leading some kind of organizational change. You go to your team describing the expected change, the circumstances leading to it, its objectives and its implementation steps. You were taught this when you were trained to be an executive, and you know how to do it. Only now, in order to keep up with the ever-increasing pace of changes, you will have to introduce a new round of changes every month or two, instead of once every few years.

"This requires extensive awareness and willingness to invest time and effort in your employees. One should remember that each of your employees is unique and has a unique mindset and perception. Each is in a different place in life and troubled by different issues. Each understands your speech differently and has different questions. The important thing in leadership is that understanding others' preferences and position assists individuals in communication and cooperation."

Now, Peter changed the display on the screen, and a second table of Herrmann's appeared.[15] "The following table is about handling changes and getting people on board with change. Notice that in order to communicate a change, one must visit each of the four quadrants and answer the questions that preoccupy people who use each thinking style. Now, let's see what each of the characters might ask about an upcoming change."

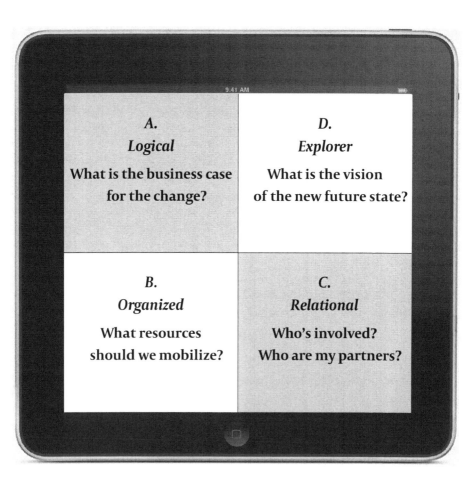

"When you speak to an A type, logical team member, you will surely have to address the issues concerning the bottom line and the facts. As an executive, he will expect to get a full definition of the goals or objectives of the change and detailed information about its financial aspects.

"On the other hand, the B type, organized team member, will focus on the resources that need to be mobilized to minimize the risk of surprises. For that purpose, he will expect to get relevant references about the specifics of the change – timeline, known risks, statistics and performance history.

"By now, you can already figure out that a totally different approach will be required in order to meet the concerns of the C type, relational team member. Above all, he will be concerned with the implications and emotional impact on him and his family, team members and customers. He will want to know who needs to be involved, who are his partners, and who will be there to listen to concerns?

"Finally, in order to get the D type, explorer team member, on board, a clear vision of the future state should be communicated. The explorer will frequently ask 'why' questions and expect to have the freedom to influence the process. As he prefers to keep his options open, he will have concerns about constraints or restrictions. He will also need to know how the change may affect his future and how it fits into the overall big picture."

"I see," I said. "But how can a single executive lead such a process so that all the employees in his team will be on his side? How can he accommodate the different preferences and needs of each employee?"

"Now we hit the bottom line," Peter said, "and that's why we are really worried here. Our conclusion is that only a 'whole-brained' or 'multi-dominant' executive who is equally capable of using all four parts of his brain, and who is capable of reacting to the entire variety of challenges posed by management, can do so. But studies show that only 2.5% of the population truly show equal strength in all four quadrants."

He looked at me and continued, "Do you see this picture hanging on the left-hand side of the wall? We got it from a good friend in Mindset Land. Notice that there is an X mark above 4 of the 10 executives. These X marks indicate the 40% of executives who wouldn't be appointed, should their candidacy be reconsidered."

"Yes, Rona told me about it, but why?" I asked.

"The reason is simple. There are quite a few managers who are still working according to old principles and are incapable of changing their work habits," Peter answered my question in a very straightforward way. "Business guru Gary Hamel described it beautifully in one of his lectures before a group of our alumni. He aroused objection among most of the business professors when he said that the era of management has ended, and the era of leadership has begun."

"What did he mean?" I asked. I probably missed the point of this last statement.

"What is the definition of management, Michael?"

"I've never really thought about it," I answered.

"Hamel argues that management is a series of processes that are capable of guaranteeing that a complex system of people and technologies will act in an appropriate manner. The most important aspects of management are planning, budgeting, organizing, manpower, control and troubleshooting."

"This definition sounds right to me, and that is exactly what I do at work every day," I said.

"I see. But according to Gary Hamel, this kind of perception about management is out of date."

"Oh, come on, what do you mean by 'out of date'? Will an executive never have to do that stuff anymore?"

"He will most certainly have to, but in a different way. Mostly, he'll have to take one more step and switch from merely being an executive to being a leader," Peter answered.

"OK, we've been talking so much about leadership. Maybe it's time for you to explain what you mean by 'leader' or 'leadership'."

"Hamel argues that leadership is a series of processes that creates organizations or adapts them to substantially changed circumstances. A leader defines how the future is supposed to look, organizes his employees according to this vision and gives them the inspiration that will enable them to get there, despite all the obstacles.

"You see, Michael, in order to become leaders, executives must work with the four parts of their brain. They must maintain their relevance and lead their organization toward innovation and success."

"And do you have such executives?" I asked.

"To a certain extent, yes, we do. And these were the ones the king spoke of, when he spoke about turning over the leadership and the key of responsibility. Some executives, who have realized that the reality has changed, now take courses, advanced studies and workshops, to develop and work on their weaker aspects.

"I think that such executives are the harbingers of the 21st century. They have already realized that they will become irrelevant if they fail to make a personal change. This is the first time that so many executives fear becoming irrelevant, even more than they fear the change itself. This is not trivial, since most of them usually resist change." Peter smiled, "We are talking about AB type executives who realized that the skills that promoted them to their current position, will no longer promote them and that they should evolve from being executives to become leaders."

"So, are these the people who are capable of making the switch, training themselves to use all four parts of their brains?"

"Yes, indeed," Peter said, "You had visited Mindset Land before you came here, so you must realize that the individuals capable of making the change are those executives with a growth mindset, those who believe that the brain can evolve and develop through learning. Obviously, a manager with a fixed mindset won't be able to make this change as he will lack the conviction required for its success. As a result, he won't be motivated enough to start such a change, and if we force him into such a process, he will most probably fail."

"And what will become of these executives?"

"Executives with fixed mindsets will soon figure out that their value proposition has diminished, and that they have become less desirable to their employers. I admit that we all initially tend toward one or two preferred thinking styles, which influence all our skills, relationships and decision-making processes, for better or for worse. Even though, as I mentioned, we are also sure that these preferences are not rigid and that most people are capable of adopting new and different approaches. It is possible to learn how to expand the variety of our behaviors and act in different styles than those we naturally prefer."

He stopped for a moment to think and continued, "We might not have a choice, and we will have to relocate our executives to Mindset Land for a few years. I only hope we have the time to do it. The king fears that if we wait any longer, it will be too late, and his kingdom will cease to prosper. You see, this is the first time in history that we are required to work with all four parts of our brain, and that our success, as well as the success of our executives, depends on it!"

The sound of an incoming message interrupted him. "One moment, please," he said, "I just received an interesting e-mail from a colleague of mine in another land, EQ Land. We believe that our answer lies there, but I simply do not have the time for this trip…"

"Isn't that the next land we were going to?" I asked Rona. She smiled and said, "It's definitely the next stop on our journey."

"Couldn't you just come along?" I asked Peter.

"I would really love to, but I have some important and urgent experiments I must conclude in the near future," he answered. "Still, I would be more than happy to receive any bit of information you can gather during your visit, if you believe it might help me and my staff to make progress. I have no doubt that our king would also greatly value your contribution."

"We would love that," I answered, feeling sad about the current state of the kingdom.

***

"What will really happen to our society in the 21st century?" I asked Rona after saying goodbye to Peter.

"Our society will have more and more expert professionals, an abundance of engineers, lawyers, accountants and bankers, for a simple reason: today, far more people go to college, and this trend will only increase. There will be no shortage of people with bachelors, masters or doctoral degrees who have studied in a system which primarily develops the left side of the brain. But today's new reality will present them with challenges that are far more complex than those of the past, those they were used to. Therefore, there will be a strong need for individuals capable of using the four parts of their brain – those who can identify the change, get people together, lead them around through a significant vision and assist in the reinvention of the organization. Today, most executives, no matter how talented, find it difficult to work in a changing work environment, in situations of obscurity and vagueness, without having a clear map of the points of interest that they should reach. These are precisely the executives who become irrelevant."

"But it's impossible to ignore the fact that these managers have succeeded so far," I said.

"True," Rona said, "but just as the king had said, the keys to the kingdom will pass into new hands. The rules of the game have changed."

"Yes, now I remember your long speech at the beginning of our journey, about globalization, economic crises and competition, leading to the fact that innovation and creativity will become important elements in every organization. You called it added value, right? You also talked about the requirement for social responsibility, regulation and the rapid technological changes which require adaptation."

"True," Rona answered, "I also said that all of these make the knowledge experts incapable of providing a full answer, and that there is a need for people with the ability to synthesize and innovate."

"Fine," I carried on, "at this point the importance of the ability of executives and employees to create an emotional link with their customers and create a relationship based on trust is clear to me. But, how do we get there? You specifically said that those who succeed will be those who use all four parts of their brains. As we have just heard from Peter, such people are rare. So what's going to happen?"

"We'll continue our journey and find out. Perhaps you will be able to help not only yourself, but an entire land!"

4
EQ Land

We arrived at EQ Land as night fell. All I knew about this land was that this is the land of emotional intelligence and that EQ stood for Emotional Quotient, as an analogy to IQ (Intelligence Quotient – the intelligence evaluation scale we are all familiar with).

Although I was exhausted, I couldn't stop thinking about the people with the tilted heads we saw in the Whole Brain Land. I kept thinking about Peter, devoting all his time and effort to this quest of finding ways to enable individuals to acquire the skills required to successfully cope with the challenges of management in the 21st century. I remembered Peter's request to fill him in on what was happening in EQ Land. Keeping in mind his hopes for what could be learned from this land, I promised myself to document the knowledge acquired here and to send him the highlights.

***

Even though I had slept for ten straight hours, I woke up tired and moody. Thinking about all the valuable knowledge I had acquired during my journey, I wondered – why did it make me feel confused and even pessimistic, rather than excited and happy?

It was now evident that in order to succeed as a manager, I won't be able to avoid developing my soft skills. I had already realized that I must put in some real effort to fill in the large gaps in my skills, and especially the interpersonal skills. But why did this understanding bring me down? After all, I had never been deterred by learning new things.

Thinking about it all, I realized that no matter how hard I tried, I would never excel at soft skills. As I saw it, I would have to be satisfied with the ambition of reaching an average level, rather than an excellent one. Mostly, I was frustrated by the thought that I will probably have to work hard and invest much time and energy, just to achieve mediocre results.

I felt like a fish out of water. I just wanted to return home to my comfort zone. I missed my wife Mia, my friends and mostly, embarrassing as it is to admit, I missed sitting at my computer with the algorithms I had left behind and the code I left unfinished.

This was my mood as I arrived at the hotel's lobby, where I met Rona for morning coffee. Rona welcomed me with a pleasant smile. She must have sensed my mood. I have no other explanation for the kind and cheerful words she had for me. She told me that she thought I had come a long way since the beginning of our journey and that she was really impressed by the basic curiosity and the sensitivity I showed with the people we met. I thanked her from the bottom of my heart. During the time we spent together, I found out that in spite of her quiet presence, she knew what I was going through and displayed quiet concern. At the beginning of our journey, I was disturbed by the fact that she didn't talk about herself. But now, I felt that she did this out of respect and with the intention of giving me the space I needed in order to grow.

"Michael, you have the morning off. You can go on your own and take a look around. I thought it would be nice for you to have some time to yourself, after taking guided and educational tours in the two previous places we had visited. Meanwhile, I'll benefit from the fact we're here to visit a friend I haven't seen in years. Go have fun, and I'll meet you for lunch at the national library."

"I understand you're proposing that I get acquainted with this land on my own in order to free myself of some fixed mindset I may have?" I asked, jokingly.

Rona smiled, "Actually, I hadn't thought about it, but it seems to me that this is indeed the point. You see? You're already living through the insights from Mindset Land. So go on, go out and have fun. And don't forget that optimism is a key factor for your success in becoming a successful 21st century manager. It's also one of the most important life skills."

I left the hotel with my tablet, intending to document life around here and add some of my insights and interpretations. I was eager to understand what the land of emotional intelligence means.

Going out was good for me, and the cool refreshing air helped me regain my spirits. I walked around a bit and finally came to a wide and beautifully cultivated park, with green lawns, outdoor games, running tracks and fitness equipment. I sat on a vacant bench and watched long-tailed squirrels running on the grass, dogs running free in a designated area, parents playing with their children and a group practicing Tai Chi. The people were pleasant and friendly with one another. Their faces showed that they were content with their lives. Based on their appearance, I judged that they were not very wealthy and, therefore, I was surprised by their easygoing spirit, which was so different from the reality that I was accustomed to.

I was busy writing my insights about this advanced leisure culture when a young woman, who had just finished jogging, sat down beside me. "Good morning," she said, smiling.

"My name is Anna, and I guess that you are a tourist, if I may say so."

"Good morning to you too, my name is Michael. And Yes, I am a tourist. What gave me away, if I may ask?" I smiled at her, surprised by her direct approach.

"Well, your appearance blends nicely in with the scenery, but your facial expressions give you away," she replied. "No offense, but it's very easy to identify tourists by their facial expressions. It always seems to me that you have only the basic ones: happiness, sadness, fear, surprise, contempt… but you lack the more subtle expressions."

"What do you mean?"

"Here in EQ Land, our nonverbal channels of communication are highly developed, and for this reason our body language shows many nuances, a wider variety of movements and facial expressions. Besides, I believe that our basic facial expression, the default one, is much happier. Tourists who come here always seem less happy to me."

"And how do you explain the fact that people feel happier here?"

"Happiness derives from a sense of success in life. At least that's how it is for me."

"Actually, I'm just in the midst of a journey, where I'm learning how to become a successful manager. May I ask, what is success to you?" I asked the obvious question.

"Oh, that is a subject for long discussions. Do you know that you can find more than 500 definitions for the word or the concept of success? Here, in EQ Land, we identify with the definition proposed by the developmental psychologist, Howard Gardner, who defined success as one's ability to set up his goals, make plans, achieve his objectives and feel satisfied and happy upon achieving them."

"I learned about him in Mindset Land; he also discussed multiple intelligence," I remembered.

"True," Anna answered, "I'm surprised you know of him, not many people outside EQ Land are familiar with him."

"Interesting," I said, "so, actually, according to his definition, the feeling of happiness is an inseparable part of success…"

"That's right," Anna answered, "and from what I've heard about other places, it appears to me that it's easier to feel success around here. Each of us sets his or hers own objectives according to personal priorities and whatever makes them feel satisfied and happy. For instance, I have a friend whose objective is to become a CEO and another friend whose objective is to raise her children and spend as much time with them as possible. Both of them invested their time and effort in achieving their objective and are considered successful." She looked at me and continued, "Here, if you consciously set yourself a goal, make a plan and achieve it, you are considered successful."

"But aren't some people more valued than others?" I wondered, "Take for example people who have accumulated more degrees, more accomplishments or higher income levels…"

"In the past, we too measured success in terms of money and titles. People were considered successful if they spent all day at the office, and if they had accumulated many assets or 'big' bank accounts. Academic degrees were then merely a way to reach prestigious positions.

"But since then, we have moved forward. Today, beyond our professional titles and financial achievements, an important factor of our success is related to our personal development. Success criteria now include the extent to which we realize our potential in various aspects of life. It's about how well balanced and comfortable we feel. Beyond nurturing careers, we emphasize emotional, physical, familial and social well-being.

"People, who set their objectives and consistently strive to achieve them, are considered successful by us, rather than people who let society determine what success is for them. If you fail to make up your own definition of success, how can you know where to look for it? How can you identify it when it comes, and how can you enjoy its fruits?"

"So, you're saying that the majority here invests in other

areas beyond their careers. What does it say about ambitions and being competitive? Are those left aside?" I asked.

"People here are most certainly ambitious, but their priorities are apparently different from yours," Anna answered. "We strive for fulfillment and success in a variety of areas, as well as in our professional lives. Our ambition is expressed by striving for satisfying and full personal lives, including our families, our friends and ourselves. We take great care to maintain our health and emotional well-being."

"Is it possible for everyone to succeed?" I asked. "And isn't it natural that some succeed at the expense of others?"

"Once again, it all depends on how you perceive the notion of success. If you measure, examine and compare yourself to others, you have a problem. Here, we have figured out that one's success doesn't come at the expense of others because success is determined according to personal criteria. Different people act on the basis of different strengths, have different objectives and are busy fulfilling different roles, which require different skills.

"For this reason, everyone can succeed if they perform their work well. We understand that we only compete against ourselves. That is the reason each of us makes the best effort to improve and strengthen personal abilities. Of course, it doesn't mean that we expect to succeed at any given moment. But it most certainly means that we can grasp a lack of success as a temporary situation that will pass."

"I get the impression that you have some background that I lack," I said. "You say that you live a full and fulfilling life here.

What's the secret of your success? And how do I learn it?"

"We have neither a secret, nor a magic spell. Our added value in life derives from our recognition of the world of emotions, and the benefit we get from nurturing it. Emotions are a language, and our parents teach us this language from the moment we are born. They show us a full range of emotions and this way we learn the nuances and have the legitimacy to use the emotions in order to express ourselves. Also, in kindergartens and schools, we emphasize the emotional world – we develop our children's 'muscles of success,' as we refer to them. These muscles connect emotion and reason or, you might say, the abilities of the left-brain and the right-brain.

"Practicing and flexing our emotional intelligence muscles enable us to process our feelings and weigh the components of emotion and intuition within our thinking and decision-making processes. This weight, as a part of rational processes, is also the one providing us with a fuller life experience. People here learn to live with a high level of self-awareness, while controlling their impulses. They practice life skills such as persistence and perseverance, and they enhance their social compatibility skills."

"I must ask you something, and I hope you don't take it the wrong way," I hesitated. "We know about a trade-off, an exchange or a compromise, occurring in the wild, when certain abilities are developed at the expense of others. I find it interesting – is it possible that one would develop higher emotional intelligence at the expense of other skills, or vice versa? I personally can attest, for instance, that my logical-technical tendency is more developed, at the expense of my interpersonal skills. Many of my Engineering faculty friends and my work colleagues are similar in that aspect. How is this manifested here?"

Anna smiled, "Is it just me or are you implying that emotional intelligence is a nice consolation prize, at the expense of IQ? Are these two qualities interchangeable, and do we have to compromise? Let me tell you, without meaning to insult, that this approach belongs to an old and dogmatic school of thought. I wouldn't argue with an example of an animal that can see better than it hears, or vice versa. But as far as human beings are concerned, you must set aside these theories, or just remain limited by narrow concepts and poor life skills.

"Just like I do, you must also know some highly intelligent individuals who are also emotionally developed, as well as others who lack both IQ and EQ. Plus, there are many in-between cases.

"Each of us can develop and refine our abilities, beginning from our own starting point. If you exercise and build your emotional intelligence muscles, you can strengthen the links between the various parts of the brain and increase the flexibility of your thinking. The connection between emotion and reason is very central – the rational refines the emotional while the emotional feeds and informs the rational. Try to remember how many times you've had a gut feeling about a particular individual even before anything was said. This gut feeling is a signal from your emotional mind, and only later does the rational mind come in…"

I had many other questions to ask Anna, but a quick look at my watch revealed that it was already lunchtime and that I was late to meet Rona.

I thanked Anna for the valuable insights she had shared with me. "I thank you for our pleasant conversation, as well," she answered. "And please excuse me if I was too preachy. I just feel that we've reached a formula for a healthy and balanced life, and I want to share these simple insights with anyone who wants to listen."

***

As I left the park, pondering over what Anna had said, I accidentally took the wrong bus and arrived at another part of the city. It took me 15 minutes to realize my mistake. When I finally asked a group of people how to get to the national library, their attitude was kind and caring and they had a great desire to help. One of them even insisted on escorting me to my bus stop, to avoid mistakes.

The bus ride took about half an hour, and eventually the driver stopped at the entrance to a large building. "This is the national library," the driver pointed toward the building. I wondered why, of all the places in EQ Land, Rona had chosen to meet with me at the library.

As I entered the large building, I realized that we had never specified any meeting place. Based on my acquaintance with Rona and the experience of our journey together, I went up to the floor where they had books about personal growth and psychology, but she wasn't there. A familiar perfume revealed her location, sitting next to shelves under a large sign: **Success in the 21st Century**.

I approached her and apologized for being late. Rona invited me to take a seat and asked, "Have you ever asked yourself how come there are so many books, and yet people never stop writing and adding knowledge on any given topic?"

"Honestly, I never thought about it," I replied.

"I believe that the reason for this is that we still have many questions with insufficient answers," Rona said. "Each time I enter a library or a large bookstore I think about all the concepts, questions, doubts, creativity and passion for discovery that accompanies and motivates writers while writing a book."

I nodded, and Rona carried on. "For instance, take the concept of success. People have been coping with the question of the essence of success for a very long time now. There are many books written about this topic yet, people still find it difficult to define success. But you know that ever since I was exposed to the concept of emotional intelligence, the word that immediately comes to mind in this context is *success*."

I told her about my meeting with Anna and about the definition she provided to the concept of success, the one borrowed from Gardner.

"Yes, exactly," Rona answered. "I also think that Gardner was able to define success in a simple and precise manner. And now, I want to ask you some questions through which we'll be able to learn about the valuable insights of emotional intelligence and the road to success in a changing world."

"What kind of questions?" I was curious.

"First, which person influenced your life the most? Second, what was special about this person?"

I wasn't prepared for this kind of question. Since I already knew Rona well enough to know that she wouldn't settle for a superficial answer, I asked for a few minutes to arrange my thoughts. Many people were and still are significant in my life, and all of them crossed my mind: friends, army officers, teachers and family members. Many fine individuals I had met throughout my life, people who believed in me, helped me make important decisions and served as an inspiration. But as I thought about it, it was clear to me which one I would like to mention: Jacob, my great-uncle, who passed away years ago. He had been by my side since I was a young boy when I emigrated with my parents, from Argentina to Israel. Without any doubt, he was the most extraordinary individual I had ever known, and his character greatly influenced my life.

I started talking rapidly, "The person who influenced me the most was Jacob, my grandfather's brother. He was a daring person who was never afraid to do the things he believed in. From a very young age, he figured out that Israel was the best place to start a family and decided to emigrate. He never waited for others to make up their minds for him, and that was his guideline in this case as well. He always made courageous and complex decisions. He was an independent pioneer who knew what he had to do in order to get what he wanted.

"He told me that when he first applied for assistance from the Jewish Agency for immigration, his application was turned down because his wife suffered from a severe lung disease. But he never gave up and was determined to achieve his goal. He wrote letters to officials at the highest levels, saying that he wouldn't give up, and that he believed that in Israel, his wife would be able to live for many years, in spite of her illness.

Eventually, he was successful, and she continued to enjoy a long and full life in Israel.

"He was one of the most determined and positive people I had ever met. He could always 'see the glass half full' and enjoy the positive aspects of each moment. He also had a talent for making everyone around him see the positive side of things, just as he did. He had a kind heart. I remember many people seeking his help, and he helped each and every one of them. I remember how much he helped my family when we immigrated too. Apart from him, we really had no one. He always told me that it was our job to help one another and to contribute as much as possible to the well-being of others. People really loved him, and everyone wanted to be his friend. I think it had to do with his unusual ability to listen. He was a very patient listener, and he knew how to analyze a situation and help the individual reach a solution.

"In all that he did, he always found the time to listen to himself as well. He taught me that we should spend a few minutes every morning in contemplation, to think about our situation and how we feel about it. Whether we were happy or sad, what we had to do in order to be happier. He was most certainly one of the most amazing people I have ever met. Many times throughout my life, I stop and think what he would have done or what decisions he would have made in my place. One of the most difficult moments in my life was saying goodbye to him when he died.

"I know how important it was for him to realize his own potential for success, so he could support himself and his family, while still learning a profession, in a new language, in a new country. He made great efforts, working and going to the university, throughout daytime and evenings, while having to improve his Hebrew reading and writing skills."

I noticed that the library section we were sitting in had nearly emptied as I was speaking. It appeared that my enthusiastic tone made people search for a quieter place. I felt slightly embarrassed, but it didn't spoil the positive feeling I was filled with as I remembered Jacob.

She smiled and said, "What an interesting story. I bet your grandfather's brother was a very special person who brought much happiness and security to the lives of his family members. You told me he went to the university. What did he study?"

"He studied medicine. He always wanted to become a doctor, but he couldn't achieve it in his homeland. When he came to Israel, he knew he couldn't begin his studies right away, due to difficulties of language and lack of financial support. But he studied Hebrew and in a short time, he knew enough to be accepted into medical school. He also worked hard and managed to save enough money to pay for it.

"When I immigrated with my parents and encountered language difficulties, he talked to me about the time he attended medical school. It was one of the most challenging times of his life, under constant pressure from demanding studies, work and family. But Jacob, as always, was able to remain optimistic and was grateful for the opportunities he had. Ever since, whenever I felt challenged, I would go to him and he would tell me about the hard time he went through during his studies, and how he was determined to succeed and make it to the finish line."

I continued my story, as the memories flooded back. "After

his graduation, he started working at Rothschild Hospital in Haifa. He was a devoted and compassionate doctor. He was the kind of doctor who would look his patients in the eye, listen to them and do his best to help them – not only at the physical level, but at the emotional and mental levels too. His patients felt as if he was there for them, holding their hand and supporting them through tough times in the hospital. Unfortunately, this is very different from what happens in most hospitals, where the doctors never look at the patient. I remember how important it was for him to get to know his patients. He understood the connection between mind and body long before it became trendy. He always said that one of the primary roles of the hospital doctors was to calm and soothe the patient, as well as reassure his relatives.

"While other doctors rested or chatted during their breaks, he would go over to the patients and their families, asking questions, telling stories, joking and helping them to relax. When I visited him at the hospital, I saw the broad smiles on the faces of his patients as he entered the room. And, by the way, when he retired, he let us all know that he wasn't the 'stay-at-home' type of guy, and he would volunteer as much as he could. It always was important to him that his life would consist of significant acts."

Rona listened and smiled. "Do you remember that I talked about emotional intelligence, when we first met?" she asked. "You said that you suspect emotional intelligence is designed to support people who could not find a more dignified job to do."

I nodded and blushed.

"Your great-uncle is a model of an individual with high

emotional intelligence. I wonder how he developed these abilities. Each sentence you said about his life expresses high emotional intelligence."

"Honestly, Rona, I still don't understand why you sanctify the link between emotion and intelligence. I learned that emotions should be kept out of your business and life, especially when it comes to making difficult decisions. Other than that, I find it hard to believe that one can actually develop these skills."

"With such an attitude, Michael, it looks like you have a pretty good chance to be accepted as a resident in the fixed and dreary half of Mindset Land," Rona said with a smile.

"But before we go on, I'd like to challenge you with another question. I would like to hear from you about a book that influenced your life, a book that changed your thinking and led you to insight."

Again, I took my time and thought about it. In recent years, with all the pressure at work, I mainly read professional literature. The two books that came to mind were *Seagull*, by Jonathan Livingston and *The Alchemist* by Paulo Coelho. Both of them were gifts from Mia, but honestly, I didn't find any personal connection or meaning in either of them at the time. I was going to answer that I couldn't think of a book that influenced me, but then I remembered Dan, my instructor in the army. He was so impressed by the book *Who Moved My Cheese?* [16] by Spencer Johnson, that he bought me a copy.

"Would it be all right if I talk about a book that impressed another individual, who was very close to me?"

"Sure," Rona answered with a smile.

"Dan was one of the most impressive officers I met during my military service," I opened my story, "an extremely confident guy, full of resourcefulness and determination. He wasn't the type to get good grades at school, but it was clear to everyone that he had what it takes to succeed. Even though he grew up in a poor family, he was also sure of his ability to succeed. Every time he heard someone complaining, he would tell him to stop complaining and see what he could do to improve things. Dan would be found reading at any given moment. There were always several books in his room. One evening, as I walked into his room, I saw him reading a book with a funny name, *Who Moved My Cheese?*"

"I jokingly asked him what had happened, and if everything was all right, and he said 'Michael, you must read this book. It's as if someone took everything I think and believe in, and put it into one book.' When we returned to the base after a week off, he came to me with a smile and said, 'I believe that if something good happens to you, you must share it with someone else. I bought you a copy of the book.' I was impressed by the friendly gesture, but I had no desire to read the book. When I finally read it, the book's messages seemed highly simplistic to me.

"Dan's enthusiasm about the book was so great that he prepared a presentation about it. One evening, he invited all of us to his room and told us the story." I imagined Rona was familiar with the story, but I briefly described it anyway.

"The four protagonists are two 'littlepeople' called *Hem* and *Haw*, and two mice, *Sniff* and *Scurry*. They all live in a maze, in which they look for cheese. The cheese symbolizes all the good things we want in life, happiness and success. After finding a large stock, they enjoy the abundance and establish a daily routine. But one day, they see that there is no more cheese. Both groups, the 'littepeople' and the mice, represent different approaches to coping with this change.

"The two mice aren't biased by prior beliefs or expectations. Actually, noticing that the cheese supply diminishes, they have mentally prepared themselves to the task of looking for new cheese. They don't panic but regard the situation as a simple problem. They tell themselves that if the reality has changed, they need to change their course of action as well. So, they set out to search for new cheese, which they eventually find.

"In contrast, the two little people, Hem and Haw, go through a deep crisis. They were both caught unprepared since they expected that the cheese supply to be constant. One gets angry and wants everything to be back to the way it was before. The other complains and refuses to go looking for new cheese, as he fears the unknown. The two of them just blame each other, waiting for the cheese to return. Eventually, it takes a long time for Haw to realize that he needs to brush aside his fears and return to the maze. He finds new cheese and leaves messages to Hem. Uncompromising, Hem stays behind, stuck in his expectations for the old cheese to return.

"Dan discussed the messages of the story, about how it was important that we stop and evaluate our situation before the cheese disappears. Our fixations might prevent us from finding new cheese, so we should develop our self-awareness and figure out what is holding us back. We should always remember that he, who won't change and adapt, will fail. If we want to find new cheese, it's important that we continually move forward, visualize ourselves finding the cheese and enjoying it. If I'm not mistaken, it's called guided affective imagery. In other words, the faster we let go of the old cheese, the sooner we find the new one.

"To be honest, I now see the connection between the things I heard from him 15 years ago and the issues we're dealing with on this journey."

Rona listened intently, and I noticed that she was also taking notes. Eventually, she said, "You've provided us with excellent examples. Your stories provided a lot of material about emotional intelligence."

She continued, "I want to tell you about psychologist Dr. Reuven Bar-On. He said that of all he had learned about people over the years, three questions interest him the most.

"The first one is – why are there people with an extremely high IQ, who have not achieved much in their professional lives and are not content with their personal lives and relationships? The second question, complementary to the first one, is – how is it that there are people with an average IQ, who achieve a great deal in life, enjoy good relationships, have many friends and professional accomplishments, lead teams and organizations, progress and earn well? And the last question, which I also find intriguing, is why do some of us enjoy better emotional well-being, happiness and optimism than others?

"Bar-On concluded that there are several groups of emotional, social and interpersonal competencies, which help us cope optimally with challenges. They also help us to identify beneficial situations and to take advantage of such opportunities. In other words, these are competencies which have behavioral manifestations related to the connection between emotion and cognition, between interpersonal and professional skills. Bar-On actually coined the term EQ as an analogy to IQ.[17]

"Prior to Bar-On, John Mayer and Peter Salovey dealt with the correlation between cognition and emotion and with the definition of emotional intelligence as a form of intelligence.[18] Daniel Goleman also studied the contribution of the abilities of emotional intelligence to management and leadership. Goleman contributed significantly to the concept, by bringing it to the general public in a book that became a best-seller and reached a greater audience and popularity."

"What is its title?"

"It has an interesting title: *Emotional Intelligence: Why it Can Matter More than IQ...*"[19] Rona said.

"However, Michael," she continued, "it's important for you to know that there are quite a few researchers who are critical of this area of emotional intelligence. One of them is Professor Zeidner[20,21] from the University of Haifa. However, he also agrees that emotional intelligence has become one of the most prominent research areas in modern psychology."

"What is emotional intelligence composed of?"

"There are some theories, but I would like us to focus on Bar-On's ©[1]. Essentially, he created a model made up of 15 subscales, which are grouped in five composite scales. Let's take a look at the tablet."

---

[1] Copyright © 1997 Multi-Health Systems, Inc. Reproduced with Permission from MHS. Derived from EQ-i Manual. Note: The EQ-i model has been updated to EQ-i 2.0. See contact MHS for details.

Intra-Personal™	• Self-regard™ • Emotional self-awareness™ • Assertiveness™ • Independence™ • Self-actualization™
Inter-Personal™	• Empathy™ • Social responsibility™ • Interpersonal relationship™
Stress Management™	• Stress tolerance™ • Impulse control™
Adaptability™	• Reality testing™ • Flexibility™ • Problem solving™
General Mood™	• Optimism™ • Happiness™

"Interesting, but how is it related to the books we talked about, or to Jacob?"

"I will soon show you that the way you described Jacob meets the definitions of emotional intelligence. But before that, let's get familiar with the emotional intelligence subscales."

The Intra-Personal Component

Emotional Self-Awareness

Emotional Self-Awareness is our ability to recognize and understand our own emotions. It is our ability to differentiate between subtleties in our own emotions while understanding the cause of these emotions and the impact they have on our thoughts and actions, as well as on others. It includes the understanding of those things that motivate and promote us, as well as those that hold us back. This subscale is the basis for all others. It is the first step toward understanding and improving ourselves.

Self-Regard

Self-Regard is our ability to respect ourselves while understanding and accepting our own strengths and weaknesses. It is often associated with feelings of inner strength and self-confidence. True self-regard is built in stages, based on real achievements and is a strong predictor of competence.

Assertiveness

Assertiveness is our ability to communicate feelings, beliefs and thoughts openly, and defending personal rights and values in a socially acceptable, non-offensive, and non-destructive manner. It is also about being open, honest, and understandable when expressing ourselves.

Independence

Independence is our ability to be self-directed and free from emotional dependency on others. It reflects our autonomy as we follow through with our thoughts, as we realize the objectives that we set for ourselves. This subscale requires a definition of our desires and an understanding of what we should do in order to achieve them.

Self-Actualization

Self-Actualization is our willingness to persistently try to improve ourselves and engage in the pursuit of personally relevant and meaningful objectives that lead to a rich and enjoyable life. Self-Actualization affects our ability to realize our own potential and capabilities. Individuals with high self-actualization skills experience richer, fuller and more meaningful lives.

The Inter-Personal Component

Empathy

Empathy is our ability to recognize, understand, and appreciate how other people feel. It involves being able to articulate our understanding of another's perspective and behave in a way that respects others' feelings. It is our ability to proactively show interest in other's feelings and thoughts, to be attentive and sensitive not only to the content of what people say, but also to the way they express it. In its essence, empathy is the ability to see the world from a different point of view.

Social Responsibility

Social Responsibility is willingly contributing to society, to our social group, and generally to the welfare of others. It involves acting responsibly, having social consciousness, and showing concern for the greater community. In the organization, this subscale is characterized by devotion, loyalty and obligation to the organization and to its causes.

Inter-Personal Relationship

The Inter-Personal Relationship subscale refers to the skill of developing and maintaining mutually satisfying relationships that are characterized by trust and compassion. It includes the desire to establish meaningful relationships and the ability to feel satisfied with relationships.

Stress Management

Stress Tolerance

Stress Tolerance involves coping with stressful or difficult situations and believing that we can manage or influence situations in a positive manner. It is our ability to constructively manage our emotions, to withstand adverse events and stressful situations by actively and confidently coping with the feelings of stress.

Impulse Control

Impulse Control is our ability to resist or delay an impulse, drive or temptation to act. It involves avoiding rash behaviors and decision making. It is also our ability to control aggressive feelings, anger, hostility and unacceptable behavior.

Adaptability

Reality Testing

Reality Testing is our ability to remain objective by seeing things as they really are (and not as we would like or hope them to be). It is our ability to recognize when our emotions or personal bias can cause us to be less objective.

Flexibility

Flexibility is our ability to adapt our emotions, thoughts and behaviors to unfamiliar, unpredictable, and dynamic circumstances or ideas. This subscale relies on the effective judgment of reality – the ability to read the changing reality.

Problem Solving

Problem Solving is our ability to find solutions to problems in situations where emotions are involved – our ability to understand how emotions impact decision making. More specifically, it includes the ability to identify and define problems, to seek and find relevant information and to take a systematic approach to solving the problems. It is our ability to creatively generate several potentially useful solutions, making decisions and implementing the chosen solution.

General Mood

Optimism

Optimism is an indicator of our positive attitude and outlook on life. It involves remaining hopeful and resilient, despite occasional setbacks.

Happiness

Happiness is our ability to feel content with ourselves, others and life in general. Happiness is also our ability to have positive social interactions and a general sense of well-being. It is to be energetic, to have fun, to enjoy good moments and to feel satisfied with our own activities.

"Rona," I said, "I understand why subscales such as stress tolerance and problem solving are essential to my success as a manager. I can even understand, after undergoing such a significant part of our journey, why the interpersonal aspect is important. But it's still unclear to me why subscales such as emotional self-awareness and happiness are important to my success as a manager in a high-performance culture."

"That's an excellent question, Michael. Let's talk about the concept of emotional self-awareness and examine its connection to management. Executives who are highly aware of their emotions understand how they feel in various situations at work. They also know how to use their emotions in order to motivate themselves and others. This helps them in many respects and enables them to understand how others feel and what can be done to assist them. It allows them to realize when they are on the edge, to stop and step back from the situation before they erupt. Also, it allows them to know that they are exhausted and that it is time to recharge, and so on.

"Larry Bossidy and Ram Charan wrote the excellent book called *'Execution: The Discipline of Getting Things Done,'* which emphasizes the importance of emotional self-awareness in executive roles.[22] Take a look at the following summary:

- Know thyself… It's the core of authenticity. When you know yourself, you are comfortable with your strengths and not crippled by your shortcomings.
- Self-awareness gives you the capacity to learn from your mistakes as well as your successes. It enables you to keep on growing.

- In no area is emotional self-awareness more important than in the performance culture which draws on every part of the brain and every aspect of being human.
- If you know yourself, you can control yourself. You can curb your ego, be responsible for your own behavior, adapt to changes, adopt new ideas and stick to your integrity and decency in any given situation.
- Also, self-control is the key to real self-confidence. It is about the positive kind of control, rather than other forms of self-control which result from weaknesses or insecurities, such as the intentional display of self-confidence or arrogance."

"I see," I replied after giving it some thought, "you have linked self-awareness, self-control and self-confidence. Now, what can you say about happiness? Why is it important for executives to be happy?"

"Notice, Michael, that both optimism and happiness are indicators of emotional intelligence. People, who function better or more effectively in most of the EQ subscales, are happier than others. Why happiness? Remember your conversation with Anna, who told you how people are influenced by other people's emotions. Studies show that the first emotion we perceive at work is the emotion of our direct manager. Happy executives make their team feel energetic, open and excited about their activities. However, if the manager is worn-down, feels bad and unhappy, his team will feel the same way: a team without energies, a sluggish team that finds everything difficult to accomplish. Happiness is the fuel of all of us. Can you visualize what such two teams look like?"

"Yes, of course," I answered, "I have a vivid picture of both…"

"After familiarizing ourselves with the various EQ subscales, let's return to Jacob, your grandfather's brother. I want to show you that your description of him fits the definitions of emotional intelligence perfectly. I have taken notes of the things you said, and now we can examine a few examples and analyze them together, using what we have learned about EQ and its subscales.

- You said he never waited for others to make up their minds for him, but always made courageous and complex decisions. These are reality testing, self-regard and independence.
- You said he was one of the most determined and positive people you knew, and that he could always see the glass half full and see the good in any given situation. Here we can see self-regard as well as optimism.
- You mentioned he had a kind heart, that he helped all who approached him, and that he always said that it was our duty to help and assist others as much as possible and to contribute to their well-being. Surely you can identify empathy and social responsibility here.
- You also said that people really loved him, that everyone wanted to be his friend, and that you think it was due to his tremendous ability to listen. This is yet another example of his empathy and interpersonal skills.
- According to your story, he said that we have to take a few minutes every morning to contemplate our feelings and think about what we should do in order to be happier. It is evident that he possessed emotional self-awareness as well as happiness.

- He also told you about one of the most challenging periods in his life, when it wasn't so easy to live for a long period of time under the stresses of studies, work and family. Therefore, he possessed stress tolerance, flexibility and self-actualization.

"We can go on and on, Michael. It turns out that your grandfather's brother was a person with high emotional intelligence."

"Yes, this is evident to me now. I admit that until now I saw emotional intelligence as something like self-assessment questionnaires in the back of women's magazines. But now, I begin to understand what it is and its connection to success."

"Now let's try to analyze the book that Dan was so excited about."

"You know, I met him about a year ago when I was doing a reserve duty activity. We talked all night long. He told me how happy he was with his life and that he has already achieved most of the objectives that he had set for himself, during his military service. It is incredible, but even though it has been 15 years, he still talks in terms of the concepts of the book, and I was really happy for him."

"Do you see a parallel between the message of the book and the insights that we're collecting during our journey?"

"Yes," I admitted, "for instance, understanding that change frequently occurs and that we should accept it, adapt and move on."

"True," Rona confirmed. "And moving on is what enables growth, which is critical for managers and employees. When a sudden change occurs, some of them will be able to adapt to it, while others will fail to adapt and remain stuck where they are. Besides, remember that no one can escape those changes. As you very well know, we are in a constant state of change in all areas: management, strategy, competition, customers, employees, technology, regulations or economics."

"So, how do you link the ability to adapt to changes with the emotional intelligence subscales?"

"It's very simple, Michael. Very intuitively, you can deduce that these are the subscales of the Adaptability composite scale – Reality Testing, Flexibility and Problem Solving."

"Now, tell me one more thing," I asked, "Can we measure emotional intelligence? Do I have any way of knowing my status in any of its subscales?"

"Yes, Bar-On had developed a self-evaluation questionnaire which was recognized as a scientific and reliable measure of emotional intelligence by the world's most prestigious institutes. It is a self-report test in which you rate yourself through 133 statements."[23]

"Wow! I didn't know this kind of discipline is measurable. Can I actually see where I am today, in terms of each subscale?"

"Yes, definitely. For each subscale, you will get a numerical score, much like intelligence IQ tests. Below a certain level, a low result will indicate that this subscale is an area of growth for you and that you could benefit from developing that skill. Your strengths will be the subscales for which you get a high score."

"That's really fascinating," I said, feeling like I would really like to try it out.

"But you should also notice a significant difference from

IQ results. Results that are too high come with a price: they mean that you are over-using a certain 'muscle.' For instance, if someone receives a very high score in the assertiveness subscale, it doesn't necessarily mean that he is highly assertive, but that he might be aggressive. Similarly, someone who gets a very high score on the empathy subscale might find it difficult, as an executive, to tell his employees things that could hurt their feelings. During feedback conversations, he might find it difficult to tell them where they should improve.

"Now, recall your last conversation with John, as well as your conversation with Martha. Can you try and analyze those according to the concepts of Bar-On's EQ subscales?"

"I'll try," I answered. "John claimed that I am insufficiently open to changes and that I tend to postpone or even oppose them in every possible way. He also claimed that I tend to rearrange reality according to my needs, failing to realize the fact that we now operate in a completely new, different and complex reality. It must have adversely influenced my ability to effectively solve problems. In terms of EQ, he must have been talking about my adaptability skills.

"In addition to my adaptability skills, Martha mentioned my interpersonal skills – my ability to listen to others, to enter into their minds and genuinely understand what they feel. I must have been really focused on my tasks, never paying attention to where my employees were. She added that my customers too were probably dissatisfied with the way I communicated with them, giving the impression that I'm not entirely on their train of thought."

"You know," I added, "now that I'm analyzing it with you, I'm starting to realize that I was quite disconnected from the people around me. I didn't give much consideration to the fact that there were others who were influenced by my behavior. I now realize that there are two gauges I have never paid attention to – the internal gauge of emotional self-awareness and the external gauge of reality testing."

"Great," Rona said with a smile, "it is incredible how much you have learned and internalized during our journey. Plus, you have begun to realize the importance that this knowledge has for you personally, as an executive and as a human being.

"Some people think that emotional intelligence was just a short-lived, late 20th century trendy concept. However, it is important for you to know that it is as significant as it was during the 20th century. In fact, emotional intelligence is now utterly critical. We are talking about a period in which change is the defining characteristic of our work environment, and this is the reason why adaptability becomes a key issue.

"For a start, don't forget the Y Generation, that now occupies a significant portion of the workplace. You know that this generation is far more committed to its executives on a personal basis than it is to the overall organization. Meaning, the interpersonal aspect is critical for leading people.

"Second, we described the current work and business environments in terms of white water rafting. This reality will demand from everyone the ability to work under stressful conditions, in an ever-changing reality, for long periods of time. That makes optimism as essential as adaptability! If you are not optimistic while rafting in white waters, it will be very difficult for you to help others stay on board and lead them through challenges."

"Another significant subscale of emotional intelligence is independence. How can organizations and executives reinvent themselves and win in a highly competitive world without high levels of independence?

"And, last but not least, don't forget our internal source of energy, our fuel, which is our happiness or emotional well-being. How can we keep on rafting without fuel? Executives who succeed over time, are those who maintain themselves and their emotional well-being."

"Yet, Rona," I said, "it appears to me that we are neglecting professional competencies. Are they meaningless?"

"Meaningless? Not at all! Professional skills are important and even crucial, of course. But they're simply not enough. I meet many talented people like you who feel cheated because they have been developing their professional skills throughout their entire lives, instead of putting some effort into developing their soft skills too. And now, they don't have what it takes to succeed and further advance in their professional careers as executives.

"Do you remember my telling you that I foresee a shortage of competent executives? As I said, there will be an abundance of executives equipped with diplomas, professional skills and experience. However, there will also be a real shortage of competent executives that are capable of managing themselves and their teams in such a challenging reality, a reality so different from the one in which they gained their experience. Today, many engineers and managers are leaving the workforce. I've met many of them, and I have no doubt that they had responded very much like Hem and Haw: they never internalized the change, while assuming that their competencies and their success are measured by the same criteria they were measured by, ten years ago…"

Rona's final statement took me back to my last conversation with John, who tried to make me realize that things are changing. I felt embarrassed as I realized that I had been in complete denial, just like Hem and Haw. "So, how do we develop emotional intelligence?"

"There are two critical conditions. The first is to have a growth mindset. The second is to internalize that it's going to be a long process which requires investment and may be painful. Unfortunately, you can't just be sedated for surgery and wake up after the procedure is over, with the doctor saying 'the operation was a success, and you are free to go,' like some executives would like it to be.

"In the next land that we'll visit, the Centered Leadership Land, we will build a model to characterize executives who will succeed in the 21st century. We're scheduled to leave in an hour."

5
Centered Leadership Land

We almost missed the flight to the Centered Leadership Land. At the last minute, we made it to the gate and boarded the plane. During the flight, I looked out the window and saw steep peaks, wide valleys, mountains and creeks. The beautiful sights from above moved me and I drifted into thoughts about the experiences we had had. For the first time in this journey, I was able to get a fresh look at them. The insights I gathered in each of the places we had visited connected and complemented each other.

Visiting Mindset Land, I learned that leaders who will succeed in the future will be those who have a growth mindset. It will be those who understand that they don't know it all, who observe and recognize the change, and who adapt themselves to it through constant learning, investment and determination. These individuals won't be paralyzed by fear of failure; they will know how to accept mistakes as part of the process.

Visiting Whole Brain Land taught me that in addition to

these qualities, leaders and executives in the 21st century will be required to use all parts of their brain. They will have to invest in the development of their weaker parts, in order to improve their learning and communication skills and use their personal abilities to the fullest.

In EQ Land, I discovered the 'emotional intelligence muscle', which provides a connection between the various parts of the brain and serves as a bridge between the logical and the emotional. Exercising this muscle creates better synthesis between intelligence and emotions in the thinking processes, and thus leads to a higher level of self-awareness. When the balance between the logical and the emotional is constant and lasting, it becomes easier to know how to act in any given situation and when to switch gears. In much the same way, this process will also promote social competencies and provide a fuller life experience, as Rona says.

These concepts were no longer gibberish to me, and I could perceive their various aspects. The concept of "soft skills" no longer terrified me. Yet, the thought that some people are able to meet all of these criteria still sounded quite impossible to me. I wondered whether there were actually such individuals who possessed all of these skills in addition to the high-level professional requirements, which are taken for granted, of course…

I started to think about the executives in my company. Pretty quickly I thought of John, to whom I owed thanks for this journey. One of the things that characterized him was infinite learning and development. He always said that leaders who didn't learn any new lessons were like basketball players who never practiced and just showed up for the games.

John was always up-to-date with the current professional literature; he had a subscription to management magazines such as The *Harvard Business Review*. He also insisted on having a professional coach. Clearly, he meets the criteria for a learning individual. But what about his personal skills, how were these expressed?

First, he was highly skilled in anything related to project development and management. He knew how to lead people and get them to do what he wanted, and he was always open to listening to others. Second, at any given moment, he could express his vision for the near future. He knew how to create a very convincing picture of where we would be in six months or a year. Finally, it seems like he was definitely using the four thinking styles – the analytic, the organized, the relationship creator and the visionary. With this thought in mind, I fell asleep. By the time I woke up, we were about to land.

Soon after leaving the airport we got to one of the most peculiar places I had ever seen. We came to a large road junction with signs to destinations such as New York, Hong Kong, Georgia, Gujarat and many others. While I was forming an impression of the cosmopolitan atmosphere, Rona indicated that we should go down a boulevard, following the road sign **Tamil Nadu**.

I was familiar with the place, as I had traveled there before my studies. But I couldn't understand the meaning of such a road sign in our current location since Tamil Nadu itself is in the south of India…

When we got there, I noticed that the place looked really authentic. We stopped at a chai shop and I enjoyed the scent of cardamom, cinnamon and cloves.

"Welcome to the Centered Leadership Land," Rona smiled. "Were you able to connect with the creative part of your brain and guess what goes on here?"

"Not really," I replied. "What is this place? How come the streets here lead to various locations on the globe, places which are so far away from each other?"

"Well, this is the Centered Leadership land and it's not a theme park, although it might look like one. This land is devoted to inspiring leaders and pioneers in many domains, from all over the world. Each street or area is dedicated to such a leader and serves as a source of knowledge and inspiration. Through the reconstruction of the places in which these leaders grew up, at the corresponding period of time, one can grasp the origin of their beliefs, ideas and actions.

"Business leaders are but a small portion of all the leaders that are represented here. You will also find well-known political leaders and human rights activists such as Martin Luther King, Mahatma Gandhi, the Dalai Lama and even David Ben-Gurion. Rosa Parks, the African-American civil rights activist from Alabama, who refused to give up her seat on the bus to a white passenger in 1955, also has a place of honor here.

"Aside from the leaders who are no longer with us, some of the streets are dedicated to the new generation of political and business leadership. Notice that these places were not created for admiration. They serve as learning and inspiration centers in which one can learn from the actions and accomplishments of great past and contemporary leaders.

"Of all the world's business leaders, I have chosen to focus on a woman who grew up in Chennai, India. Let's hurry and catch a rickshaw to the neighborhood where she grew up."

We went out of the chai shop and into the vivid and crowded Indian street. We caught a rickshaw and passed busy markets, impressive antique sites, little temples from which incense smells emerged, street restaurants with steamy pots and wandering cows. I enjoyed the rhythm of the place and the beauty, mixed with the stench, the noise and the soot. As we entered a suburban neighborhood, the driver announced, "Here we are!"

We paid his fee and got out of the rickshaw.

"So, this is the childhood neighborhood of the woman I've chosen to focus on. Would you believe that this is the origin of one of the world's most highly esteemed executives?" Rona asked.

I looked around and saw gray houses with inner courtyards, next to a basketball court. This wasn't a slum, certainly not by Indian standards. It was definitely a middle-class neighborhood.

"This is where Indra Nooyi was born and raised. She is the current Chairperson and CEO of the food and beverage corporation PepsiCo and a very influential woman. Unfortunately, I don't know her personally, but I'm a huge fan of hers."

"I've never heard that name. How did you find out about her?" I asked.

"This is an excellent question and one that shows what a long way my profession has come… If, in the past, we would focus mostly on our areas of expertise, today, we must pay attention to what goes on in our business in general. Moreover, we shouldn't settle with observing the business in our country alone, but all over the world. As a consultant, I try to follow leaders of the business world and learn about their actions. That's why I keep myself updated with professional literature, magazines, and conventions all around the world.

"I first saw Indra Nooyi at the World Economic Forum,[24] a convention of international political and business leaders such as prime ministers, chancellors and leading CEOs, which is held once a year in Davos, Switzerland."

"Have you ever had the opportunity to participate in one of the Forum's conventions?" I wondered.

"No, the participation cost is very high. But YouTube is free, and you can watch the best lectures at the convention. Two years ago, I watched a fascinating session about the future of leadership and the challenges of organizations in the 21st century. This session was held by HSBC Chairman Stephen Green, Google CEO Eric Schmidt, China Mobile CEO Wang Jianzhou and PepsiCo CEO Indra Nooyi.

"The four leading CEOs talked about one of the most interesting points in today's business world. They discussed the fact that economic models have begun to change. During the previous century, a simplistic capitalist concept ruled, according to which the objective of a business is to make as much money as possible, as fast as possible. However, during the first decades of the 21st century, maximizing profit for shareholders is no longer the sole objective. Business success is now measured in terms of business viability, having a stable value and human infrastructure, serving the whole of society. These four CEO's talked about the central questions that each organization should ask itself. The first is – how do we nurture innovation and arrive first at the best ideas, in order to keep on growing. The second is – how do we find the most competent executives and retain them?"

"But there are so many powerful and inspirational CEOs," I said. "Did you pick Indra Nooyi because she's a woman?"

"You're touching on another interesting point, Michael, but that is not the reason I chose her. Indeed, for the first time in history, we are seeing more and more women in key positions in senior management, including CEOs. It's possible that this, too, is a result of global changes. However, I chose Indra Nooyi for the same reasons that *Fortune Magazine* has named her number one on its annual ranking of *'Most Powerful Women in Business'* for five consecutive years, from 2006 to 2010. She's been one of the world's top five leading women for many years. This is a woman who heads a thriving global corporation with an annual turnover exceeding USD 64 billion. Can you imagine that? This amount is much higher than the annual budget of many countries around the world. Still, this isn't why I chose her; many CEOs have increased the profits of the organizations they manage. As far as I am concerned, there's something special about this woman and her management style, thanks to her ability to connect the capitalist-materialistic world with the world of values.

"Indra Nooyi participated in the convention in Davos in the following year as well, in a panel discussion on the future of business organizations and, primarily, the way they are perceived by consumers and by people in general, as well as the role played by organizations in the economic crisis."

"In this session, Nooyi turned to Professor Michael Porter of Harvard, a leading authority on competitive strategy, with harsh words about the training that CEOs and senior executives receive at business schools around the world. According to her, these institutions neglect aspects of social responsibility and long-term thinking. They raise generations of executives who ignore the needs of the environment and the society in which they operate, due to their desire to achieve short-term benefits. She stated that the mantra of business schools – 'worry about the next quarter' – wasn't valid anymore."

"But the desire of executives to make immediate profits is very natural, isn't it?" I said.

"True. To Nooyi, this desire also comes naturally, or else she would never have succeeded in leading the world's second-largest food and beverage company, while significantly increasing its revenues and net profit. Still, she says one should aspire to long-term thinking by caring for the environment, the community and the well-being of the employees. She claims that doing so actually provides justification for short-term profits."

"And does she implement her principles?"

"Definitely. She does more than talk; she also practices what she preaches, unlike certain CEOs, whose actions don't comply with their words. Since joining PepsiCo in 1994, she has built a whole new strategy for the organization. Under her leadership, PepsiCo started promoting and focusing on healthier products such as natural juices and fruit-based energy snacks. Nooyi also set objectives to improve the health benefits of PepsiCo's products, following criticism leveled at PepsiCo and similar corporations about their contribution to the obesity epidemic around the world."

"Unlike CEOs of other organizations, Nooyi wished to turn the harsh criticism of the corporation she managed into an opportunity for learning and growth. Only a CEO with a growth mindset can do this. She gathered all her senior executives and asked them to become their own critics, as well as listen to those who criticize them, to understand their claims and improve themselves. Later, she summoned her own harshest critics. She told them that even though PepsiCo did not take responsibility for obesity in the United States, they would do their part to encourage a policy that would fight obesity and would promote healthy products. She made those commitments despite much criticism from the shareholders, who are less interested in public health and more interested in profit margins. When asked about her policy at a press conference, Nooyi said – 'We invest lots of effort in giving our customers healthy products. Should I regret this? I am proud that we have changed our state of mind.'"

"And how is this related to success of executives in the 21st century?"

"Slowly and gradually, we will understand the connection. It isn't trivial," Rona said. "One of the things Nooyi repeats, whenever possible, is that the set of abilities that are important for success in the 21st century would be very different from those required in the past. She came to this conclusion after traveling the world and holding many conversations with various executives at PepsiCo and other leading global organizations. Also, she often talks about a 'turning point' as the world becomes ever faster-paced. By the way, according to her, the turning point occurred in 2007.

"It is important that you understand, Michael – Nooyi is not only an executive, but a true leader. She doesn't make do with the existing organization and meeting schedules. Instead, she initiates, leads people through situations of uncertainty and creates changes in a dynamic reality. In many interviews, she is asked what leadership is. She always answers that it is a difficult concept to define and that good leadership is even harder to define. But she has a simple test: if your men are prepared to follow you to the end of the world, you are probably a great leader."

"How can you develop leadership if you are not Indra Nooyi or one of the world's leading executives?" I asked, "Is it even possible?"

"Some strategic consulting companies try to provide executives and organizations with tools and insights regarding the road to leadership. In 2009, a groundbreaking research paper was published by Barsh and Cranston,[25] two consultants from McKinsey: *How Remarkable Women Lead*. Based on interviews with dozens of leading women executives, they constructed a leadership model called centered leadership, comprising five dimensions that will aid in building the skills and strengths on the road to leadership."

"You just said that they interviewed women. Are their conclusions also valid for men?"

"Definitely, the centered leadership model was adopted by many researchers as a model characterizing leadership among both genders. For instance, two senior consultants at McKinsey, Keller and Price, published a fascinating book about the ability of organizations to succeed in the 21st century. They adopted the centered leadership model as a key for leading organizations to success."[26]

"Now you've got me," I said, "what is this model?"

"Technically, the centered leadership model comprises **five dimensions**. These dimensions are interrelated in the sense that each strengthens the others. We will study them together, from up close, to see how the model provides executives of all ranks with tools to help them lead in a gushing white water reality.

"When I was first introduced to the model, I wondered: who of all the leaders today is a living example of this model? I had no doubt that this was Indra Nooyi. To me, her way is the essence of the best in each dimension of the model.

"Now, let us delve deeper into each dimension and consider its contribution to the success of leaders in the 21st century. We will start with the first characteristic: **Meaning**. Barsh and Cranston argue that the sense of meaning enables leaders to motivate themselves and the rest of the employees at the organization. Leaders with a high sense of meaning feel committed to their work and strive to realize their objectives out of passion and enthusiasm. They are aware of their strengths. They use them and inspire others to do so as well."

"And according to your stories so far," I noted, "Indra Nooyi is undoubtedly a CEO with a great sense of meaning."

"True. And apropos Nooyi, in the context of the meaning dimension, the first thing I would like to tell you is about the objective-oriented performance methodology she introduced – *Performance with Purpose*. From the beginning of her career, she realized that in order to get people to come to work satisfied, or even happy, there should be an added value, beyond the financial profit. This added value is the sense of purpose and direction, or as it is referred to in this model, meaning.

"She started to implement this methodology, based on the two aspects of the meaning dimension. The first aspect is the **personal meaning**: It is important for each employee to bring his whole self to work, to be authentic and to find the things that are personally meaningful to him. This will result in the organization and the employee both giving their best to one another. The second aspect is the **organizational and social meaning**: It is important that the organization considers aspects of social responsibility and long-term thinking – the understanding that each action comes with a consequence. Every organization acts within the human society and should strive to perform processes that are beneficial to society, rather than abusing it and its resources."

"Do you know if the use of this methodology of meaning in the organization had actually influenced employees?" I asked.

"Certainly, all aspects of the Centered Leadership model have been studied and surveyed by McKinsey.[27,28] Based on 2,000 executive's self-assessment of their performance and satisfaction, McKinsey discovered that '*finding meaning in one's activities has the strongest impact on general satisfaction*' and that it is '*five times more influential than either of the two closest dimensions*'.

"At the bottom line, each and every one of us requires a sense of meaning at the personal and collective levels in order to arrive happier to the workplace and to make his best effort. In interviews and lectures, Nooyi said that she is convinced that the sense of meaning motivates not only herself but also her senior executives, their subordinates and, eventually, the entire organization."

"It would be interesting to learn how the shareholders relate to the process of meaning led by her…" I wondered.

"Make no mistake, Michael, the growth of the organization is Indra Nooyi's primary interest, and she knows that this is the center of her business. But she also understands that in order to get there, and stay there for a long time, additional processes should be put in place. According to her, organizations that favor the profit line won't be able to retain it for long, even if they do achieve a positive balance. As far as she is concerned, business success means a wide and well-based moral and human infrastructure and the establishment of such a sense of purpose and meaning, throughout the organization.

"You should know that most of the researchers studying motivation nowadays agree that it is the end of the era of the 'carrot and stick' approach. Motivation in the 21st century is first and foremost a derivative of a deep sense of meaning."

"It takes a lot of patience and learned optimism to invest money in organizational projects which will only bear fruit in the future," I pointed out.

"True, and this leads us to the second characteristic of the centered leadership model, **positive framing**. This dimension enables us to take a constructive and more beneficiary look at reality and to raft forward, even when things are rough.

"This is most certainly a prominent characteristic of Nooyi's leadership, and I think that we need to return to her biography in order to understand this. After earning her master's degree in Chennai, India, she applied for a scholarship to Yale. She arrived in the United States alone, with only $50 in her pocket. And, by the way, when she mentions this in her interviews, she laughs and says that if her parents had believed she would actually get the scholarship, they would most probably never have encouraged her to leave home...

"Nooyi worked as a receptionist to support herself during her studies and saved every cent. This is a woman who immigrated to a foreign country on her own, and who lived far from her family and friends in difficult economic conditions. There is no doubt in my mind that her ability to positively frame difficult situations assisted her on her road to success."

"I wonder if she is using this capability now, as CEO of a large international corporation," I said.

"Sure," Rona answered. "After all, the business world is extremely volatile, especially at a time of such frequent cycles of economic crisis. As CEO, she has to cope with failures, declining sales, layoffs and harsh criticism from the shareholders. It is not that she didn't realize the difficulties and the hardships. But, being the CEO, she knew that she shouldn't manifest any signs of anxiety or distress. Although she had a realistic grasp of the situation, she also knew that giving up is unacceptable. She understood that the management has to identify the growth opportunities and convey optimistic information about these opportunities throughout the organization. She refers to the attitude of seeing the glass half full as 'realistic optimism.'

"You know very well that many people lost their jobs during the recent economic crisis. PepsiCo employees were also worried and wondered about their own fate. Nooyi realized that the mood she instills at the organization would have an immediate effect on the executives and employees, especially on their productivity. Therefore, she positively framed the situation. She conveyed a strong message throughout the company that things were all right. She justified her optimism by pointing out the fact that they were a consumer staple company, which would not be affected much by the crisis, since people still buy food, even during a downturn."

"Do you think that this optimism, this positive framing, is a trait she always had?" I asked.

"From interviews given by Nooyi, it is evident that the feelings she carried from home were that there would be no limit to her accomplishments in life. Her mother instilled the belief she could achieve whatever she wanted and encouraged her to dream big. Growing up with parents like these most definitely has a tremendous influence on you."

"This reminds me of the insights from EQ Land, when we talked about Jacob and his learned optimism," I noted.

"True. Many people believe that learned optimism is a kind of manipulation by individuals who are not bright enough. I can tell you without a doubt – pessimistic individuals suffer from laziness of thought. It is so easy to see what is wrong, what is not working, what could go wrong. As an advisor, I say it to all the managers I work with, as I try to teach them to focus on what is currently working and what may succeed in the future. This is a critical ability, required for the continuous success of any organization or individual.

"Make no mistake. In a changing reality such as ours, in the eye of the storm, one of the most important abilities of a leader is to properly read and face the changing reality as it is.

On the other hand, it is equally important for a leader to instill learned optimism in his staff. The leader must show faith in his staff and their ability to win despite the temporary difficulties they face. Learned optimism makes a substantial contribution in any change process, Michael, and especially in significant ones. After all, if you don't believe that success lies ahead, why even try?"

"I would like to remark, Rona, that the two dimensions of the model you mentioned so far, sense of meaning and positive framing, sound to me like characteristics you either have or you don't."

"This is arguable, and the world's best researchers, including Martin Seligman, would disagree with you. But let's get to the third dimension, which most certainly can be developed and perfected. This characteristic is named **connecting**, and it means the active construction of an array of connections with other individuals, within and outside the organization. It's well known that people with a larger and more complex social network enjoy better terms at work. They make more money, get promoted faster and derive greater satisfaction from their work."

"This is also related to what we've learned in EQ Land, and particularly to interpersonal abilities," I said.

"You are right. You should also know that Nooyi argues that emotional intelligence is the most important competency for leaders. And this comes from a woman who regularly appears on the lists of most influential woman in the world and tops the list of most influential CEOs.

"Now, let's examine her performance in the context of

connecting with other individuals. What is noticeable about her is that she has a vast network of connections with CEOs, senior consultants, heads of state and regulators. However, when asked about the main skills that are important for a CEO, she always answers that it is the ability to connect with talented and young employees. She talks a lot about Generation Y, about their constant need to be on the move and switch jobs for promotion. According to her, executives who are capable of associating themselves with their young employees by adding an emotional touch, will be able to retain their excellent employees."

"Of course," I answered.

"Michael, I think Indra Nooyi is a CEO who knows the extent to which people are a central component to the success of the organization. She doesn't use this knowledge in a cynical way, as many executives do."

"How do you reach this conclusion?"

"Here is an example: after getting the job as CEO of PepsiCo, she went to her hometown in India for a party her mother was throwing in her honor. She was excited to meet her friends and family, in her new position. The interesting thing was that the guests who attended the party came first to her mother, and not to her. They congratulated her mother and showered her with compliments and admiration for having raised such a wonderful daughter, who brings honor to Chennai and to all of India. That day she realized that parents, who work so hard raising their children, making sacrifices, caring for their well-being and for their success, are not acknowledged when their children finally do succeed.

"She decided to put this understanding into action. Upon returning to the United States, she wrote a personal letter to the parents of her executives, in her own handwriting, describing their achievements, activities and contribution to the success of the organization. She also wrote about the things that PepsiCo does to help make the world a better place. With a smile, she says that many of the parents responded with gratitude. You can surely imagine what it felt like for the parents to get the letter, and consequently, how their children, the senior executives, felt."

My first reaction was that it sounds quite embarrassing… "Wow, I try to imagine my mother receiving a flattering letter about me from our CEO. She'd be very pleased although it feels awkward. Still, Nooyi surely sounds like an extraordinary executive in terms of her concern."

"I agree. And it is this kind of concern that drives her employees and creates motivation. It is what increases their sense of capability and achievement, and gives them a feeling that they are worthy and indispensable, thus enhancing their commitment to the organization and its objectives. It may surprise you that motivation is not related to the size of your bonus, but rather to the sense of meaning and to your relationship with your manager. Her caring and concern are related to the fourth dimension of the model, named **engaging**.

"The concept of engagement incorporates commitment and involvement. It is our ability to listen to our inner voice, to trust ourselves, to initiate and act without the need for approval, and to get others to act under conditions of uncertainty and risk. And what are the conditions of uncertainty and risk, Michael? Most of the conditions today are just that."

"And how is this dimension manifested with Indra Nooyi?"

"Indra Nooyi says that she is stern and demands a lot from herself, and this filters into her environment and eventually raises the bar for all those around her. According to her, only individuals who take complete ownership of their development and organizational activity can lead an organization to success over a long period of time. According to her, as CEO, you lack the privilege of resting on your laurels. CEOs must constantly learn and develop since reality is constantly changing. Nooyi believes that we should always aspire to be the best and to be aware of the fact that this requires a never-ending process of learning and evolving as a part of an executive's daily life. One who fails to do so will probably be incapable of maintaining his competitiveness over time.

"She sometimes jokes about the fact that CEOs don't have a written guide to teach them how to manage an organization with a turnover of USD 10 billion, 20 billion or 50 billion. They are forced to write the book as they work. As CEO, she is expected to make difficult decisions under conditions of uncertainty, and this requires great physical and mental efforts. She doesn't sleep more than four and a half hours a night, and most of her time and energy is spent on leading organizational strategies.

"Indra Nooyi is definitely an involved CEO. She's highly in tune with the organization she heads. In her own words, 'I am a walking ad for PepsiCo.' She never hesitates to go down to the manufacturing floor, for a close examination of her business decisions. A great example of her approach could be her trip to China before PepsiCo entered the Chinese market. She went into houses, stores and restaurants in order to become intimately familiar with Chinese consumption habits."

"And what do you mean by mentioning the ability to listen to your inner voice?" I asked.

"She's not afraid to think differently, and says that each and every one of us has a compass that should direct him and his actions. She is well aware of her strong influence on her organizational environment, as well as on her social-global environment. She uses any platform she can to present her beliefs, and argues that one of the roles of global organizations is to cooperate with governments and make the world a better place."

"Rona, you said she once insisted on promoting healthier products, in spite of the reservations of the members of her board. I assume that this is what you mean when you speak of listening to your inner voice."

"Exactly, Michael. I'll give you another example of her commitment to her principles and of the fact that she doesn't bow down to external pressures. During her first year as CEO of PepsiCo, the members of the board expressed their dissatisfaction with the expense of implementing the methodology of objective-oriented performance. She didn't panic, but stayed loyal to herself and to her own path. Her answer was that this was the only way she knew to manage a corporation on the scale of PepsiCo."

"I can understand the members of the board," I noted. "Like any group, they also fear changes, especially when these changes also cost so much…"

"But remember that striving for change doesn't mean that you're pushed to it by being unsuccessful. It means that you're always searching for ways to learn, to continuously improve and make yourself fit for the changes imposed by reality."

"Honestly, Rona," I confessed, "from the picture you're painting here, I would never want to trade places with her. You said yourself that she gets only four and a half hours of sleep a night. It sure sounds like she has no life outside of work. What about leisure, family outings, friends, hobbies?"

"Right you are. I also ask myself how she and other executives of her status manage to survive for so many years in such a demanding position that doesn't allow you any time for yourself."

"So, how do you explain it?"

"It has to do with **managing energy**, the fifth and last dimension of the model. Understanding how to manage and channel our energy is a key factor in our actions and in gaining emotional well-being. As I said before, it isn't necessarily related to money, but to resources such as leisure, friends and more.

"With such a demanding job, it's hard to say that Indra Nooyi has an abundance of emotional well-being. However, any knowledgeable individual understands that it's impossible to work for a long time at her pace without maintaining and creating energy. I believe she has a few ways of achieving this. First, like any executive, she understands that when we choose a demanding career, it comes at a price. But even in this demanding world, she is capable of taking care of herself."

"How?"

"First of all, by just looking at her, it appears that she really enjoys what she's doing. When we're dealing with things we love and are good at, there is a sense of flow."

The word 'flow' reminded me of the spiritual experience of

people returning from India, but as Rona continued I realized this wasn't what she meant.

"The concept of 'flow' was defined by psychologist Mihaly Csikszentmihalyi,"[29] Rona continued. "Flow is a state of complete absorption with the activity at hand and the situation while feeling that nothing else matters. There is great pleasure when we delve into this kind of activity that takes us to the point where time just flies by and we forget anything else, undisturbed. In such a situation, we're completely submerged in the moment, and our performance is enhanced. In addition, after we complete the activity, we don't feel exhausted, but charged with energy."

"I can certainly understand what you are talking about," I pointed out. "I also love my job… But what else keeps Indra Nooyi going for so many years as CEO?"

"When asked what the secret of her success is, she always answers that it is her family, friends and faith. Indra Nooyi is married and is raising two daughters. She has a circle of friends, and she also has faith. These are the sources of her energy."

"Well, she sounds like a real wonder woman," I smiled.

"I know it sounds too good to be true, but believe me, she is indeed exceptional. She's a combination of hard skills and soft skills, high cognitive and strategic thinking abilities, along with high emotional intelligence. I have no doubt that many are those in the business world and business schools that find her unusual, as I do. She inspires whoever listens to her and to her principles, which are also the ones that she lives by.

"When she was interviewed for an article about the requirements from executives in the 21st century, she said that as far as she was concerned, it was a privilege to head the organization she was leading. She said that every day, on her way home, she asks herself what was it that had earned her the privilege of being CEO, and what new things she has learned. I believe that each and every one of us should ask himself these questions, whatever position or path he chooses to define his success."

"I recognize that she is indeed a remarkable woman," I said. "But I must say that the combination of abilities as you describe them, definitely sounds critical for CEOs. Yet, I feel that it is less critical for middle management and even for most senior executives. We don't need to manage everything, and we most certainly don't have this kind of influence or impact which is typical of the work of a CEO such as Indra Nooyi. For this reason, I'm not entirely convinced that the model of centered leadership is relevant to me."

Rona looked at me for a long time. "We are nearing the end of our journey, Michael. At this point, you should be able to answer your questions on your own, rather than wait to be given answers. Take a few minutes and try and think of the five dimensions of the model in your own personal context. This exercise could assist you as you go back to work."

I thought about it for a few minutes, and then I shared my thoughts with Rona. "The first dimension I can think of is **connecting** with other individuals. At this point, I realize that this is one of the most required abilities for success, not only to CEOs, but also to middle managers like me. Any manager must connect with others: his subordinates, his superiors, his consultants and interfaces at other organizations. I remember that John asked me to work on a project with an executive from a large global corporation, and it was a complete failure. In the aftermath, I realize that this failure derived from my inability to connect with him on a personal level. I had no clue, at the time, that what really mattered were the relationship and the mutual obligation that follows."

"That's a beautiful and excellent analysis. What about the other dimensions?"

"Regarding **positive framing**, as we have said all along, leaders today handle an extremely challenging reality, which is charged with uncertainty. In my daily work I, too, have often encountered situations in which it appeared that we had gone back to square one. Occasionally, it even seemed that I reached a point where I had absolutely no idea what could be done. I remember seeing Ron, one of my colleagues, talking to his team and motivating them, explaining that if they took the right measures they would be able to succeed in spite of all the difficulties. At the time, I thought he was deluding his staff by making unrealistic promises. Today, I realize that it is learned optimism that allows us to continue 'rafting' in spite of the difficulties. I understand that an important part of my job as a leader, in order to improve situations, is to emphasize what works well in addition to what does not. You need both to describe things as they are.

"Regarding **engagement**, I must say that up to now, this dimension only guided me in the professional aspect. Now, I realize that I must expand it into other aspects, interfaces and processes. This understanding has accompanied me from the first land we went to. When I'll go back to work, I intend to delve into the project and take responsibility for all of its interfaces. I am not only talking about management aspects, but also about my vision and my ability to connect with other individuals. I intend to take full responsibility for my development and learning process. I realize it's important that I make myself heard and say what I think, especially when my vision is different from everybody else's. Deep down, I know now that I'm capable because this is the difference between a significant manager and an irrelevant one."

"What about the **meaning** dimension?" Rona asked.

"I must honestly say that I have never considered the sense of meaning, neither did I ever consider it as an element related to my success at work. Now I understand that success, in any area, will belong to those who actually strive to accomplish their goals, those who don't give up in the face of difficulties. Over time, in such a challenging reality as we live in, full of obstacles, you won't go much further if you don't have a sense of meaning to guide you. So, with those understandings in mind, I've started to formulate my own sense of meaning, dividing it into organizational meaning and personal meaning, inspired by Indra Nooyi.

"At the organizational level, I know that the products we develop significantly improve the quality of life for heart patients all over the world. It definitely gives us all a strong sense of meaning. At the personal level, as a manager, I'm thinking about my team members. It's evident to me now that my role as a leader is to instill in them everything I have learned on this journey. Among other things, I must instill the growth mindset and the importance of developing emotional intelligence.

"Up to now, the only sense of meaning I was able to appreciate was related to ambition – to succeed by being promoted to the next position and making more money. Today, I realize that if I find meaning in more internal aspects of my self-development, it will lead me to whatever I wish to achieve.

"And about the final dimension, **managing energy**, I associate it to what we talked about in EQ land, about how feelings are contagious. I can remember those managers who came to work filled with vitality and positivity. We all felt like them when working with them. Others arrived at work drained, and this made us feel that way too. If I want an upbeat, energetic team I have to work on my energy levels. The first thing that I want to do, when we get back, is to swim. I couldn't find time for this since my last promotion. But before that, I used to wake up with energy and enthusiasm and go swimming for an hour. I remember that it certainly made me feel much more energetic and vibrant. I also want to spend more time with my wife, Mia. Today I realize that if I do this, it will certainly improve my ability to go to work the next day with higher levels of energy.

"Being energetic is also related to the sense of meaning we talked about before. Remembering how I really love my job and how good I feel about it, I can feel many moments of flow, just like Csikszentmihalyi had mentioned. This sense of flow is also a source of energy.

"I also know that when I feel energetic, it is easier for me to dare and face new and challenging issues, even in the face of my fears. As a leader in the 21st century, I will most certainly get bogged down managing my energies."

6
I-21

"And now, Michael," Rona said, "I have a surprise for you. We have spent so much time talking about the infinite journey of executives toward success in the 21st century. Now, before going on to the fifth and final land in your private journey, you have a once in a lifetime opportunity to see yourself in five years' time."

"You mean I should write a summary about where I would like to be in five years' time?" I hesitantly asked.

"No, no, I mean you can actually **see** yourself in five years' time. We are going to visit the hi-tech labs of FutureSym, the inventors of a unique simulator capable of showing you yourself in the future, based on your current characteristics; a kind of a virtual realization of a future reality. When we get there, a technician will give you a helmet and connect you to electrodes reading your data. The simulator will evaluate your readiness for management in the 21st century."

After a rather long trip, we reached the labs. We went into a dark and cozy room, where we met Patrick, the technician, who greeted me with a large smile. "You're lucky, Michael. You have a rare opportunity to experience your life five years from today."

I asked about the connection between his work and the concept of "vision" and whether the option to clearly visualize it would make it more attainable. Patrick thought for a moment, and said, "This process is indeed based on studies on the power of vision. It means that if we can imagine a reality in a detailed manner, our chances of getting there are multiplied. The helmet you are about to put on will make you see your thoughts five years from today as if they were a movie. You'll actually be able to see what you're thinking!"

Suddenly, I was afraid. What if I didn't like what I saw?

Patrick read my mind and said, "Look, the process works in a way that lets you start whenever it's convenient for you. Normally, your thoughts will wander at first, and it will take time to calm them down. When you feel you can focus them and tune-in to the future, you can press the red button and start seeing clear images."

He connected me to the electrodes. My heart was pounding. It took about 20 minutes until I felt I could press the red button and start watching myself five years from today. I took a deep breath, focused and pressed the button.

The first images were very similar to my life before I set out on this journey. I remembered what Rona told me about changing mental maps, took another deep breath and focused on our journey together. The experiences of the four lands we just visited went through my mind. I remembered the people, the sights and the smells, and then I dared to take another look at the simulator.

The image became clearer. A complete day in my life, five years from now, passed in front of me. At first, I saw myself at the head of an oval table with another 20 team managers and employees leading a debate about a big and significant project. I noticed the positive atmosphere in the room, the open conversation. It was apparent that everyone enjoyed their work. I saw how each and every one of the participants felt comfortable saying what they thought, and how each and every one of them assumed personal responsibility for the project. At the end of the meeting one of the team managers came to me and asked me, with regard to our mentoring session, whether we could meet sooner than scheduled because he had some urgent matters to discuss with me.

Next, I saw myself meeting a strategic client in the senior management meeting room. The client, a CEO of a large company, talked about the anticipated hot projects. From time to time he asked for my opinion regarding one process or another, which has been implemented in his organization. His look conveyed honesty and sympathy, from which I understood that I had been able to build a significant relationship based on trust and proximity with this man and become his trusted advisor.

In the next image, I was leading a major change at the company. There I was, standing in front of all the division's managers and employees, applying the four thinking styles, trying to answer my team's questions in the most effective language for each participant. I was talking about the vision of the change, about the reasons for changing our objectives, about schedules, about figures, about the emotional consequences of the change for each and every member of the staff and for our clients. I saw myself positively framing the situation at hand, or in other words – doing my best to lead the boat through the white waters.

Eventually, I saw myself leaving work at the end of the day, content and satisfied, eagerly anticipating the rest of the day with Mia and our two children.

I had no idea how long I was wearing the helmet – whether it was one hour, five hours or a whole day. I left the room and saw Rona, looking intrigued. "How was it, Michael? Were you able to see yourself in five years' time?"

This was the first time throughout the journey that words failed me. "It wasn't easy, but yes, I did it. It was a fascinating experience."

"And how are you feeling?" she asked with interest.

"I have mixed feelings," I answered. "On the one hand, I really enjoyed watching the leader I am about to become. But, on the other hand, I'm not sure that I have what it takes to actually become such a leader."

Rona smiled, "I'm happy that you got to see yourself in five years' time and that you liked what you saw. This simulation definitely points to the fact that you are on the right track. It confirmed what I had thought from the start – that you have what it takes to become a true leader in the 21st century."

I was surprised. "How come you never told me that before? Had I known you had faith in me, I would have felt more secure, and this entire journey would have looked different…"

"The answer to your question is related to the final, fifth land, **I-21**."

"I-21?"

"Yes, with the meaning of '*me in the 21st century*.' From this name and its meaning you can understand that **I-21** looks different to each and every one of us. All the insights gathered in the lands we went through lead to our own **I-21** land and are expressed through our personal, professional and organizational activities."

"Wait, so actually… You don't need to travel a long way to investigate it?"

"Actually, to get a proper look at it, you simply have to go back home, to your daily life. In two hours we will board a plane back home. Upon returning to your daily routines you will start a journey to the most fascinating land man can ever reach. Each and every one of us can go to numerous beautiful places, but no journey is as exciting as the journey of self-discovery, self-development and self-creation."

"In that case, I understand that the journey through **I-21** is not limited in time…"

"True. The journey through your personal land never ends, and it is obvious that as you begin it, you will understand that everything we went through was just a setup for the real deal. You return home with insights providing you with a good starting point for orientation. Just remember that this is not a mere toolbox, as there is no ready-made toolbox for the 21st century. The key is flexible and adaptable thinking, enabling dynamic balance. In the past, people went through various processes to 'find themselves' in order to find a direction in life. In the 21st century, this is insufficient. In order to succeed, people will have to 'reinvent themselves' and even 're-engineer themselves' once in a few years."

"I'm starting to envy explorers like Columbus and Marco Polo… They set out to the unknown as well. But at least their goal was evident to them – new lands, natural resources, commerce routes, new cultures…"

"This is the point. In the 21st century, our unexplored areas won't be physical. Therefore, in order to succeed, people will have to reinvent themselves and make a similar process in the organization they work in."

"And how am I supposed to do this?"

"This is a challenging process which requires plenty of awareness, investment and perseverance, but I believe that you're already equipped with the tools needed to go through it."

"I'm already aware; that's for sure. But what entails investment and perseverance?"

"The way to remake ourselves begins with a simple **mirroring process**. In order for the process to be effective, it is important to make it a routine, part of your everyday. Throughout the process, you must clear half an hour of your time, at the end of each day, and recreate the day you went through and the meaningful events you took part in. Choose a place where you feel calm and ask yourself a few questions, based on the lands we have visited:

- In which events throughout the day did I display a growth mindset and in which events did I stick to the fixed mindset?
- Did I use all four parts of the brain – the analytic, the organized, the relationship builder and the integrative?

> Which of my brain tendencies were more dominant, and did they serve me well?
- Which EQ subscales did I use today? Which mental muscles served me? And at the same time, which muscles are relaxed and need strengthening?
- Did I emphasize the five dimensions of the centered leadership model and did I develop the skills and the strengths required for a leader in the 21st century?

This daily mirroring process is the investment required for you to stay on the right track. Perseverance means that you have to keep on doing that as a habit for life, just like your decision to swim daily."

These many questions echoed in me. I took a deep breath. "I understand that I am supposed to remake myself. But who will be there to help if I get stuck? Who will assist me in practicing the growth mindset, sharpening the four parts of the brain, exercising the relaxed EQ muscles, and acting according to the five dimensions of centered leadership?"

Rona apparently understood the source of my worry and answered in a relaxed voice, "first of all, I think you are going to need far less help than you think. And second, you have Martha, John and me. We'll continue to assist you on your journey toward becoming a leader in the 21st century."

"Even the daily mirroring process looks demanding, Rona. The questions you posed sound heavy, and it's not clear where I can fit them into my tight schedule…"

"I agree with you, the mirroring process is demanding at first. But in a few weeks you will begin the coaching routine, and by then it will take less time and become a sort of daily inventory. I guarantee you that it's worth the effort because this is the key to providing your edge over others.

"In my eyes, self-development is a mandatory tool enabling you to see yourself clearly and examine your progress, to identify patterns managing your life, to know your skills, your fears and your barriers. Observation of these issues will enable you to develop to a higher level of self-awareness and to find the patience in your stressful routine. The mirroring process will assist you in understanding when to lead and when to stay behind, when to take responsibility and when to learn to trust others. It will also show you how to become an authentic person. Authenticity, Michael, is overwhelming. It makes you the person everyone wants to do things with, no matter what. This will naturally reflect on your personal life, your children and your *joie de vivre* in general."

"Rona, I'm still trying to figure out why you didn't tell me, at the beginning of the journey, that you believed in my ability to succeed and to lead. Did you want me to find this out for myself?"

"Exactly. I didn't tell you what I thought as I strongly believe that one of the most important talents for a leader is to lead oneself. The need for reinforcement is natural, of course, since we all like compliments and kind words from those around us. But these words cannot be the source of our motivation. As a leader, you must develop your own sense of significance, security and clarity that will enable you to act without depending on constant approval from everyone. And that is what you did on this journey. You've undergone a meaningful personal process, without expecting support and reinforcements. Your achievements are all yours, the process is real and noticeable and now, you do get positive feedback. But that feedback is not your source of energy, not your fuel. Getting, or not getting reinforcement, is not the only factor to motivate or paralyze you, because you have yourself and your own insights."

"Yes, I'm beginning to figure that out…"

"And now, Michael, it's time to go back. I have no doubt that the mental process you went through on this journey will assist you in creating your own **I-21** land. Let's grab a taxi to the airport. We wouldn't want to miss our flight. There are plenty of people waiting for you at home."

7
Back to Work

Rona definitely convinced me of the importance of this **mirroring process**. On the plane back home, I took my calendar to clear half an hour out of my schedule, every evening, assigning it to a daily follow-up process. As Rona recommended that I sit in a quiet place, I immediately thought of Café Ana, our neighborhood café, with its pleasant simplicity. For years, since I was a student, this cafe has been my favorite spot. As a person who loves coffee shops, I got to sit in many other places, but Café Ana is my home port. I go there whenever I'm searching for a quiet and private place in the heart of the city. I sit at a table facing the window or on the comfortable couch, and after the first sip of my cappuccino, I can feel a sort of flow, accompanied by productivity and creativity. Certainly, this was the place where I should do the daily mirroring process.

I returned to work two days after Rona and I excitedly said our goodbyes, promising each other we would meet again. The return from my fascinating journey wasn't trivial. I admit that I couldn't sleep all night long, due to my excitement over the first day back to my "normal" life. Lying awake in bed, I revisited the people I met, the scenery I saw and the experiences I had during my journey. I was curious to see how my staff and colleagues would greet me. I missed everyone, and I was filled with joy and curiosity in view of the expected meeting. I was eager to implement all that I had learned on the journey. But I also promised myself I would not be like those who have "seen the light" and have this urge to express their honest opinion over everything.

In the parking lot, in front of the building, I felt I was back. I walked inside and went up to my floor. Everything looked the same, but the feeling was different. I took a fresh look at the colorful paintings in the halls, and I noticed the great effort that was put into designing our offices. The colors reminded me of the first half of Mindset Land. Many questions raced through my mind during those moments. First and foremost, I wondered whether I really was successful in my journey. I wondered whether it would be possible for me to change my old habits, to think and act in a different way over time and to implement all that I had learned. Would I become a worthy leader?

On the flight home, Rona and I had a long conversation. I remember she emphasized, over and over again, that this journey was infinite. The work that we do on ourselves should be something that shouldn't stop at any point. She also said that if we did a good job, we could feel it; as something inside would feel different. I had no doubt that part of me had already changed, but I still needed someone or something to indicate that I was on the right track.

The meeting with my team was exciting. They were happy to meet me, and it was obvious that they had missed me. After having coffee together, hearing old and new jokes, I asked to speak with each and every one of them in private, to know how they had managed in my absence. Throughout the conversations, I felt that my speech was different and that I was using the terms that I had acquired throughout the journey. I asked open questions so I could learn about their status and about their ability to 'make it' in the changing world of the 21st century. Thus, I could learn what should be improved, and how I could support them. I noticed that, unlike before, a significant part of the conversation revolved around personal issues, some related to work and some not.

Slowly, after the obvious suspicions dissolved, they started to cooperate and respond, to open up and to share. It seemed as if they were eager to have a meaningful conversation with their manager. This type of conversation had never existed before.

I have always cared deeply for my team, and this had not changed. But, in addition, I felt a much greater sense of responsibility, for them and their career development. Following the journey, I understood that I had a personal responsibility, as their manager, to see that they undergo the changes in an effective manner and that they were not left behind.

During the conversations, I realized for the first time that Harry, my most brilliant engineer, had a fixed mindset. I saw how it "bogged him down" in various processes at the organization – with the software interface, with quality assurance and with the top management. For the first time, I realized that the very fact that our most talented engineer had a fixed mindset was an obstacle to innovation, hindering our efforts to improve our products. After being exposed to his rigidity of thought, I suddenly understood why everyone opposed to his ideas although he was smarter than all of us put together. Since I was familiar with his many professional traits, as well as with his strong ambition to be promoted, I couldn't help but feel a sense of missed opportunity. I realized that nothing could be done at the moment to promote him, even though he was highly professional. Thinking about ways to help him, I realized that nothing could help Harry more than a journey to Mindset Land for him to realize how much he could benefit from leaving his comfort zone and developing a growth mindset.

Then, I noticed how Sophia, a highly motivated engineer, arrived every morning with a smile on her face. I also noticed how beautifully she worked with others, how remarkably open she was to feedback and how she often asked for it from her collaborators. I saw how she set challenging objectives and left her comfort zone without any effort, how she invested hours in setting goals and achieving them. I admit that I didn't appreciate her properly before my journey; neither did I give her much attention, as she appeared less brilliant than the others. But now, I rediscovered her, understanding that she has what it takes to succeed – a sense of meaning, positive framing, readiness for effort and investment, high-level interpersonal ability and the ability to dare, to take chances and to grow. These are all of tremendous importance when one is trying to succeed in the ever-changing reality of the 21st century.

Now, I had a feeling that Sophia could be an ideal partner in the process that I was about to lead among my staff. I knew for sure that she was the most suitable candidate for promotion. She proved herself to be persistent in making efforts on getting better and more professional. In this context, I recalled the story about the "ten-thousand-hour rule" that Rona told me and about the players at the Berlin music academy. I decided that I must tell it to my staff.

During a conversation with Ethan, a development engineer, I saw that his interpretation of the project's status derived from a "left-brain" dominance. I noticed that he lacked the ability to answer any question about his staff at the personal level, neither to address the issues that bothered each of them. I saw how he relied solely on facts and figures, with an attitude of constant close-up examination of everything, checking feasibility, searching for certified proofs. His complete ignorance of the ideas and feelings of others and his inability to coherently communicate his thoughts and connect them to the bigger picture were also evident. Ethan undoubtedly required plenty of help to successfully progress and change his attitude. Clearly, visiting Whole Brain Land would be very relevant for him. I was excited about my new ability to assess my employees and help them.

Not an hour went by, and I had already received a long e-mail from one of our strategic clients, with a serious complaint about Joel, another member of my staff. The client wrote that he was satisfied with the technical aspect of the project, but highly disappointed with the service and attitude of Joel and that he wished to have him replaced. It wasn't the first time that a client had complained about a member of my staff. But now, the source of the problem was clear to me, as was the process that I should go through with Joel. In the past, we tended to treat clients as a nuisance, bothering us on our way to create the perfect product. Now, I finally realized that it was the client who paid my salary at the end of the month, and for this reason I should find a way to offer him a winning value proposition. I invited Joel to meet me over coffee, to share some of the insights I had acquired in EQ Land. I knew that we had to do our best to be the clear choice for our clients.

As time went by, I realized that I was able to see each and every one of my staff, and especially myself, in a new light – a light originating from the lands I had become acquainted with, during my journey. The staff meetings I held in the past, which had focused on professional objectives and technical details, now seemed highly incomplete and one-dimensional; they lacked essential information necessary for the success of us all. I decided that I must start thinking about ways of making the staff meetings more significant, so that they could successfully lead us, as a team, through the white waters that lay ahead. I started planning the steps necessary to help my team members adopt a growth mindset, use skills from the four parts of the brain and incorporate their soft skills on the job.

In view of the events and the conversations I had with my team since my return, I realized that there was still much work ahead. I felt I had been given a gift, and that I must "Pay It Forward". So, I opened the first folder for the coming year on my computer and named it **"The Five Lands Journey with My Staff."** Then, I opened a new document and started typing; I wrote down all the insights that I would like my staff to internalize.

Prior to my journey, I asked Rona, how would I know that I

had passed the journey successfully? Now, her answer echoed – "You will know it once you can't keep all the insights you have acquired to yourself; when you have a tremendous urge to share with the rest of the world; when you come back to work and strive for all your nearest and dearest to internalize these insights; when you don't understand how it is possible to think or act otherwise. Then you'll know you have successfully taken the journey and have become a leader fit for the 21st century."

For the first time, I got a fresh look at my job and realized the scale of its complexity. It was obvious that I would continue to need orientation and support, and the first person I could think of was Martha. I also realized that I had to use all my insights in a deliberate way and to start the change in my staff, using all the emotional intelligence skills I could use. I should create a situation in which they would like to go on such a journey with me without deterrence or resistance. Therefore, I felt like I needed as much help as I could get.

I remembered the anger and frustration that engulfed me after my last meeting with John, when he said that I needed help and direction if I wanted to be successful. At the time, I tried to postpone getting help, as it seemed like admitting failure. Now, I yearned to receive more advice, in order to manage myself more effectively and wisely. I was glad and felt fortunate for getting this opportunity for a change. I also experienced an entirely new sensation of being thankful to John – thankful that he literally forced me into this fascinating challenge. As I walked toward John's office, I looked forward to meeting him.

"Welcome," John said as I entered his office. He greeted me with a hug and a smile. "I had a long talk with Rona and Martha, and we concluded that you were one of the best 'travelers' in recent years. You should also know that not all executives survive this journey. I'm sure that your management experience will now be entirely different, as will our next feedback session.

"You know, five years ago, I went on that same journey too. I went through similar experiences, and I also felt the need to share them when I returned. I would be delighted to schedule regular meetings to share our insights and to exchange our impressions."

As I returned home to Mia, I knew that the change I had gone through in my journey wasn't limited to the workplace, but continued through my personal life. Those same insights were just as relevant to my relationships with Mia as well as with my family, friends, acquaintances and service providers. The ability to accept the diversity of people, to learn from each and every one of them, to understand that my feelings affected my entire environment, to stay optimistic in times of pressure and assertive enough to get things done without offending others – these were all as important outside work as they are at work.

In the past, I felt like an illiterate with no direction in this new world of skills which I didn't understand nor appreciate. Now, I feel that I have the tools to succeed in it. As I started to think passionately about the challenges I was facing, I realized how everything was connected. Surely, I could make a significant contribution to my team and to the division in which I work, be successful and lead them forward. Filled with feelings of significance and satisfaction, I promised myself that I would keep developing and maintaining the insights I had acquired.

I will do that to keep waking up every morning just like I did today – enthusiastic and energized. The true journey had only just begun, but I had the appropriate toolbox to succeed, I thought as I walked to Café Ana…

Q&A:
Theoretical Background for Success in the 21st Century

- 🌀 **Mindset**
- 🌀 **Whole Brain**
- 🌀 **Emotional Intelligence**
- 🌀 **Centered Leadership**

Mindset Land

Questions for Thought and Reflection

Think about and explain to what extent you agree (or disagree) with the following statements:

1. Our abilities are innate talents (hereditary), and there is nothing we can do to change them.
2. Failure is not the end of the world; however, remaining stagnant in one place, unwilling to make any effort, is indeed a failure.
3. Through passion, enthusiasm and hard work, it is possible to attain great achievements.
4. It is highly important to try to conceal (or disguise) our flaws so that the people around us will think we are successful.
5. People are constantly changing and evolving. If you don't – you will become irrelevant.
6. One shouldn't do something new, unless he's at least 90% sure he's going to succeed.
7. It is highly important to make efforts to make others think of us as smart, talented and successful.

Mindsets

"Just as organizations are going to be forced to learn, change, and constantly reinvent themselves in the twenty-first century, so will increasing numbers of individuals. Lifelong learning and the leadership skills that can be developed through it were relevant to only a small percentage of the population until recently. That percentage will undoubtedly grow over the next few decades."

- John Kotter

1. **What is the meaning of the term "mindset"?**

The term "mindset" originates from decision theory and general systems theory. According to Professor Carol Dweck, from Stanford University, a mindset is the set of assumptions, views and attitudes of an individual (or group of people), which determines the manner in which they view and interpret situations and respond to them.[30]

A mindset is essentially our mental roadmap, telling us what to do and how to act in any given situation. Being an inclination or a habit, a mindset is also described as a "paradigm" or mental inertia. Our mindset is the result of many factors such as the way we were raised by our parents, our schools and our environment (society), with their values.

2. **Who coined the terms of fixed and growth mindset and on what basis?**

The term was coined by Professor Carol Dweck, based on more than 20 years of research.[31] A substantial part of her work was done in schools, where she observed and compared successful and failing students.

She discovered that the most prominent characteristic of successful students is their perception regarding "wisdom" and "intelligence": they believed that both could be developed. Most of them were confident that their skills and achievements consistently improve as they put in more effort – trying harder, asking questions and practicing. However, the failing students believed that wisdom and intelligence were innate skills, which they could not influence. They thought that no matter how hard they studied or practiced – they would always get the same results.

In other words, the successful students believed that they could influence the situations that they face. They believed that effective handling of challenging circumstances would lead them to success. However, the failing students felt helpless, unable to influence their fate and believing that they were destined to fail.

Carol Dweck argues that our mindsets deeply influence our achievements in all stages of our professional and personal lives. She calls these two concepts *Fixed Mindset* and *Growth Mindset*.

3. How are the two different mindsets related to the world of management?

While some executives believe that leadership is an innate skill which cannot be improved, others argue that leadership is an acquired skill which may be developed by putting efforts and getting orientation.

Apparently, this is part of the same old debate about whether we are a product of nature or nurture. Today, most researchers agree that we are a product of both. However, the interesting thing about what Carol Dweck discovered is that any individual's answer to this question has a direct impact on his or her achievements in life! This renders the "correct" answer to the old debate entirely irrelevant.

In summary, the mindset of executives, whether fixed or growth, deeply influences their achievements in both their professional and personal lives. Their attitude differentiates between those who become whom they wish to be, capable of achieving their objectives, and those who do not.

4. *What are the basic concepts of individuals with a fixed mindset?*

- **Skills and talent:** Individuals with a fixed mindset believe that their mindset, skills and behavior are hereditary and permanent, which cannot be changed or developed.
- **Success:** Success proves that they are smart and talented. It enables them to get as much external positive reinforcement as possible about what and who they are.
- **Failure:** Situations like rejection or dismissal are experienced as failures. Failure proves that they are incompetent.
- **Investing effort:** People who are competent, do not have to put any effort. Such effort would expose their flaws and show that they actually lacked the required skills to accomplish their tasks **successfully.**

The result:

These are people who spend their lives – at work, at school and in relationships – searching for validation of their intelligence, personality and character. They assess themselves in every situation: will I succeed or will I fail? Will I be perceived as wise or stupid? Will I feel like a winner or a loser?

In situations of failure, these people "fall apart." They deduce that they are not worthy because "they didn't make it" and that it is futile to keep on trying. They fear challenges and do not believe in the value of their efforts.

Eventually, they will be afraid to leave their comfort zone and reluctant to undergo or accept any significant change. At that point, they would do anything to hide their disadvantages while, at the same time, they would invest much energy to convince everybody around them that they are extremely talented.

5. *What are the basic concepts of individuals with growth mindsets?*

- **Skills and talent:** Individuals with growth mindsets believe that they will be able to nurture their essential qualities and succeed – through desire, dedication and effort.
- **Success:** Success is measured as the ability to broaden their horizons in order to learn and develop.
- **Failure:** Remaining stagnant in one place, unwilling to put in any effort to fulfill one's own potential.
- **Effort:** Development through self-challenging, learning and training, throughout one's life, are the keys to success.

The result:

Individuals with growth mindsets believe that each and every one of us can change and evolve. They see life as a journey and believe that what they do not know today, they will learn tomorrow or the next day or the day after…

They believe that the real potential of an individual is unknown and that it is impossible to predict where one might end up. This belief creates passion for learning and development, for seeking challenges and overcoming disadvantages, instead of concealing them.

For them, an expert is just an individual who made every possible mistake in a very narrow area. As a result, he would always be seeking to find a way to step out of his comfort zone. He neither desires nor needs to prove that he is talented, and invests his time and effort in constant improvement.

6. What are the characteristics of executives with fixed mindsets?

- They neither believe in their own ability to change, nor in the ability of others to do so. Therefore, they reject any change or request to improve on their weaknesses.
- They fear challenges and do not believe in the value of their efforts.
- They fear failure and being perceived as incompetent. Therefore, they "play it safe" by only doing what they're sure to succeed in.
- They are worried about how they are perceived by others

and consequently seek constant and significant positive reinforcement.
- They will do all they can in order <u>to be perceived</u> as smart, talented and successful.
- They believe that any organization has superior and inferior individuals, and they will do everything to prove their superiority.
- They let their ego manage them in their relationships with others.

All this is liable to:
- Have an adverse effect on their effectiveness and performance at work.
- Increase their general lack of trust and resistance to change.
- Limit their creativity, innovation, and problem-solving abilities.
- Have a negative impact on their health, happiness and emotional well-being.
- Make them less and less relevant to the organization.

7. **What are the characteristics of executives with growth mindsets?**
- They believe that everybody is capable of improving and developing. Consequently, they invest considerable effort in developing their own "self", as well as that of their subordinates.
- They see problems and challenges as opportunities and consistently invest considerable effort to overcome them.

- They learn from their mistakes and failures.
- They are open to criticism and encourage feedback.
- They often seek new and challenging experiences.
- They are attentive to everyone around them (executives, subordinates and consultants), since they believe that people can learn from everyone.
- They communicate with those around them with respect and as equals.
- In stressful situations, they employ a sense of humor and optimism.
- They succeed in spite of the difficulties.

Therefore, individuals with growth mindsets:

Know that not everyone can be an Einstein, but they are also aware of the fact that their potential is unknown in advance. They believe that training, enthusiasm and a passion for what they do, can lead them to extraordinary achievements. They are aware of the fact that avoidance of training, development and growth might hinder the realization of their potential as leaders, senior executives, scientists or champions.

8. *Is it possible to develop a growth mindset at any age?*

Certainly! People can develop a growth mindset at any age. The first step is recognizing the two different mindsets and the heavy price people with fixed mindsets pay for their beliefs. After all, we are talking about beliefs, and one can most certainly change them. Peter Heslin delivers a workshop for executives, and he asks the participants to answer certain questions and perform certain tasks, such as:

- Think of at least three reasons why it is important to realize that people can actually develop their abilities. Prepare a five minutes lecture for your team.
- Think of an area of weakness, for which your performance was weak in the past, where you perform better today. Explain how you brought about the change.
- Write an e-mail message to a hypothetical protégé or apprentice who is in a difficult spot in his career, sharing examples of how you dealt with challenges in your career and proposing ways to develop his abilities.
- Recall when you last saw an individual learning to do something he never thought he could do. Think about what happened, how it happened and what does it means.

9. How are mindsets related to the success of executives in the 21st century?

As discussed above, the 21st century is characterized by many rapid changes, more than ever seen before. The most important ability one can have in a changing reality is the ability to learn and adopt new habits, new patterns. Executives will be required to leave their comfort zone and expand it on a regular basis.

Executives with fixed mindsets will soon find out that their value proposition to the organization is decreasing, since they object to any process involving significant change or learning, particularly in regard to their own abilities. These executives do not perceive themselves as "inventors" and will not be able to help their organization reinvent itself and win in a competitive world. The road toward the unknown, with the possible failures that lie ahead, is perceived by them as almost traumatic.

On the other hand, executives with growth mindsets will invest considerable effort in studying and developing new areas. They will dare to leave their comfort zone and creatively assist the organization to reinvent itself whenever necessary. They will do so themselves, as well as lead their staff along the same path, to adopt a similar approach. These executives will lead successful changes.

10. How is the mindset related to the success of changes in organizations?

When John Kotter wrote his first book, *Leading Change*,[32] only 30% of organizations were able to execute effective changes. Today, almost two decades later, hundreds of books and thousands of articles later, these statistics are still valid. How come? The answer probably lies in the ability to implement the change.

In his 2008 book, *A Sense of Urgency*,[33] Kotter argues that the biggest mistake of the traditional model of leadership relies on its basic premise whereby leadership is an innate skill, "a divine gift of birth," rather than an acquired one. He says that this perception is not in line with his own observations, after 30 years of research and experience with organizations and individuals. According to Kotter, this early model does not take into account "the power and the potential of lifelong learning."

When Kotter talks about the 21st century, he adds: "In the

twenty-first century, I think we will see more of these remarkable leaders who develop their skills through lifelong learning, because that pattern of growth is increasingly being rewarded by a rapidly changing environment."[34]

Today we know for sure that if we focus only on the behavioral aspect of the change, we will probably be wasting our time and energy, because **the behavior of executives and employees is a result of their mindsets.** However, we also know that changing the behavior of individuals is the most significant challenge for business organizations trying to compete in a world dominated by changes and tremors. Therefore, in spite of the difficulty of changing one's mindset, it is the only way to create a real change.

11. How can executives help their employees develop a growth mindset?

Executives have great influence on the shaping of the mindsets of their employees. In order to establish and reinforce a growth state of mind in their teams, executives must create the atmosphere that supports it in a number of ways:

- Setting a personal example and serving as a model for the behavior of an executive with a growth mindset.
- Remembering that talent is not the most important thing about employees. Rather, what matters most are the attitude and the effort they put into their tasks. Thus, they should be rewarded for their efforts, learning and determination.
- Encouraging their staff members and creating a sense of security when they face difficulties.

- Encouraging their staff members to take calculated risks in order to be creative, think 'out of the box' and create the next trend.
- Responding to failures of staff members as opportunities for learning and development – conveying the message that this is not the end of the world.
- Developing a training program based on the organizational strategy and the employees' objectives, focusing on the skills that are important for success.
- Establishing personal development plans together with staff members. Defining their current status, the objectives to be accomplished throughout the quarter and the measures required to achieve them.
- Providing quarterly feedback to each staff member, emphasizing attitude, effort, determination, creativity and the willingness to take chances (at the risk of making mistakes).

12. *Is there such a thing as an organizational growth mindset?*

Definitely! Mindsets exist at the organizational level as well. An organizational fixed mindset is one of the reasons that many executive development programs fail to achieve their goals, even though hundreds of thousands of dollars were invested in them.

In organizations where a dominant fixed mindset is displayed, those who return from training are often discouraged from implementing what they've learned. They hear remarks from their managers, such as *"What we do here is real life; forget all those classroom theories that you have just learned and come back to the reality."* Such responses by senior executives negatively affect the behavior of their subordinates more than anything else. As a result, they relapse and resume their old habits or convey to their own team members a message which is counter productive to the necessary changes and to the organization's best interests.

On the other hand, in organizations where a growth mindset dominates, managers and employees know that development and learning are important. They also realize the need to proactively adjust to a changing reality. Consequently, such organizations invest in the design of change processes and appropriate training programs.

These programs must be aligned with the organizational strategy and its objective and must provide tools, skills and proficiencies to help people go through the change. Further, any such program must start at the top to be successful since senior management must energize the process and support any new practices. Such support should be reflected in their actions, as well as in their interactions with their subordinate executives and employees, upon their return from their training. A growth mindset organization continuously devotes resources to secure its future and its objectives.

Recently, the Harvard Business Review has published an article called *'How Companies Can Profit from a "Growth Mindset"'* which extends Carol Dweck's work on mindset from individuals to organizations.[35]

First, Dweck and her colleagues studied the existence of an organizational mindset and found that companies do possess "a real consensus" which forms a collective mindset of employees. Some companies are characterized by a belief that their employees have a certain fixed amount of innate talent and cultivate a culture of "star" performers. Other companies hold an opposite view and regard talent as a dynamic property, the result of learning, practice and experience.

Following this result, the characteristics of each type of organizational mindset were studied. Among the surveyed issues were the workers' satisfaction, levels of collaboration, innovation, ethical behavior and more.

The fixed mindset companies were found to foster a culture in which only the "star" workers get recognition, credit and reward. The other employees felt less valued, less "backed up" and were, therefore, less committed. The price that such organizations pay was striking, starting from keeping secrets to cutting corners and cheating.

On the other hand, in the growth mindset companies, the employees were found to be more committed to the organization and willing to pursue innovative projects. They were more collaborative and spent less time on politics.

13. How is an organizational mindset created?

Mostly, the organizational mindset is created and passed on without words or intention. A good example is a famous experiment which is described by Gary Hamel in his book *Competing for the Future*[36]. This experiment demonstrates how experiences from the past and present become a future behavior or tradition.

Four monkeys were put in a cage. From the top of the cage, bananas were hung, and it was possible to reach them by climbing a staircase. However, a water hose sprayed a strong stream of water at the monkeys whenever they tried to climb to the bananas. A few days later, the monkeys gave up on their attempts. At this point, the researchers disconnected the hose and replaced one monkey with a new one. When the 'new' monkey noticed the bananas, he tried to climb the stairs, but the other monkeys pulled him down, to avoid the water splash. Finally, as the monkeys repeatedly prevented him from climbing to the bananas, the 'new' monkey stopped trying, although he didn't understand the reason.

Gradually, over the following weeks, the researchers replaced all the monkeys with 'new' ones until there were no more monkeys who actually witnessed the water splashing. The researchers continued to replace old monkeys with new ones. Even though no one knew the reason (the water hose, which was removed), whenever a new monkey tried to climb and reach the bananas, the other monkeys pulled him down. They had all learned the rule – you must not attempt to get the bananas…

A similar phenomenon occurs in organizations: employees avoid acting in a way that might improve performance, just because they are used to the way things are done, while any other way is considered wrong!

14. *How can an organizational mindset be changed?*

It is important to understand that it is impossible to change a mindset relying solely on facts that are different from those that shaped the mindset. When facing facts that contradict our beliefs and mindset, we label them as wrong, irrational, unnecessary and even silly.

In his book, *Changing Minds*[37], Gardner points out six R's – six leverage points for change that have to work together in order to change the mindset:

- **Reason:** When we try to influence others, it is highly important to provide them with a reason for the change.

- **Research:** One should present evidence – based on relevant studies, supported by numbers and, if possible, on statistical analysis too.

- **Resonance:** Creating an emotional bond – people need to feel that the change is right for them in order to foster positive feelings about it. Therefore, they have to be connected through emotions: by presenting the desired idea, point of view or vision through a story.

- **Re-description:** A multi-dimensional presentation – a different opinion (or a new different point of view) is more convincing if it is presented in various ways: by a story, graphs and open questions. The various ways support each other.

- **Rewards:** Even after the need for a change of mindset has been established and accepted; even when people are emotionally connected with the leader of the change and the new concepts – one must wisely use resources and rewards (material and other) to support the new way.

- **Real world events:** This leverage is outside our influence. It includes worldwide events that might influence us all, such as recession, natural disasters, war or peace and prosperity.

Objections

It is important to remember that since mindsets are created when we are young, it's hard to change them and, naturally, there will be objections. Only when the six leverages work together in harmony will the pattern start to change.

Questions for Mirroring and Development

1. When was the last time you really left your comfort zone? In what circumstances?
2. What ability, which is important for your success, did you develop over the past few years? Who helped you?
3. When did you last feel like you were failing or didn't succeed in doing something? How did you cope with it?
4. What really excites you? How is this excitement expressed?
5. What are your prominent weaknesses at work? Who, other than yourself, recognizes them? And, how do you cope with them?
6. People are constantly changing and developing; when you look around you, which individual underwent the most significant change over the past two years?
7. When did you recently dare to do something in a new and innovative way?
8. In which areas are you putting in most of your effort at work?

9. What did you think and how did you react when you came across the following situations:
   - Another executive in your group is being praised for an accomplishment.
   - As part of a feedback process, you are told that you must significantly improve particular skills.
   - A direct subordinate of yours wants to tell you his thoughts about the last project.
   - You are coping with a task (or project) in which you have no idea where to begin.
10. If you had to describe, to your son or daughter, the importance of having a growth mindset for his success in school or at work – what would you say?

Whole Brain Land

Questions for Thought and Reflection

Think about and explain to what extent you agree (or disagree) with the following statements:

1. There is a strong correlation between the occupation we chose and our brain tendency.
2. Our brain preference may be an asset or a drawback, depending on the situation.
3. Each of us can strengthen the weaker parts of our brain by exercise and practice.
4. Our professional and personal success as managers relies only on the left, cognitive side of the brain, while our success as leaders requires the use of all four parts of the brain.
5. Understanding the preferences of other individuals assists us in communication and cooperation.
6. To a great extent, the ability to retain employees and customers is dependent on the emotional skills that are based on the right side of the brain.
7. In order to develop our weaker aspects, we require a growth mindset.

Whole Brain

"The brain is the most complex thing we have yet discovered in our universe."

- James Watson

"21st century organizations need not just half a brain – but a whole, full, complete brain, where both halves work in unison and harmony."

- Umair Haque

1. What does the concept of "whole brain" mean?

When discussing **the whole brain** concept, we are essentially talking about the division of the brain into several physical (as well as conceptual) segments. However, there is more to the concept than brain structure. Above all, it is about how one's ability to effectively use all parts of the brain will lead him to a fuller realization of his potential and much greater success.

Basically, the "whole brain" concept relies on and develops from studies of brain function lateralization (the physical division of the brain into two hemispheres, each characterized by different functions), aiming to describe and understand different thinking styles which are complementary to each other.

Therefore, in order to introduce the "whole brain" model, we first need to understand the two hemispheres concept and related model. Daniel Pink, in his book *A Whole New Mind*, phrased it as follows:

- **The left, analytic and rational hemisphere** is related to the analytical and logical abilities, language and arithmetic, factual information and time perception.
- **The right, metaphorical hemisphere** is related to abstractions and associations, identification of nuances, fitting data into the bigger picture, interpretation of sensual data and handling spatial functions.

According to this model, people have different ways of absorbing and processing data, which influences their decision-making and behavior. Our thinking style (and consequently, our mindset) reflects the dominance that a certain hemisphere has in our thinking processes. Also, as stated earlier, our mindset influences our abilities, our relationships with ourselves and our environment, and our decision-making process.

Although overly simplified by "pop" psychology, the model is useful in describing different tendencies which are related to different functions of different parts of the brain, and, therefore, to different thinking styles.

2. ***Who created the whole brain model, and what was the model based on?***

Ned Herrmann, a trained physicist and musician, took the theory of the lateralization of brain function and developed it into the whole brain model.[38] He developed his model while serving as head of the administration studies department at General Electric, where he had to cope with issues that concern all executives: how to increase employee productivity, motivation and creativity.

First, Herrmann relied on thorough studies about the different specialization of functions related to the left and right hemispheres of the brain, which results from the longitudinal fissure (which separates as well as connects them to each other). Then, he expanded the model by adding an additional dimension which results from the well-documented specializations of the cerebral cortex (which is responsible for cognitive functions) and the limbic systems (which is related to memories and feelings).

Thus, he created a four-quadrant brain model, each of which results in a different thinking style, and therefore different reasoning skills and different interaction styles with others. The proportional use of these four thinking styles shapes our mindsets and our approach to solving various problems.

It should be mentioned that the above-mentioned theories of the brain reflect a metaphor for how individuals think and learn. Use of that metaphor brought later criticism by brain researchers for being overly simplistic.[39] However, this metaphorical construct has proven useful in many organizational contexts, such as education, business and government.

3. What are the components of the model?

The integration of a second dimension to the two hemispheres model results in a four quadrants model, and therefore, four patterns or styles of thinking and behavior.

Each of us has one or two dominant thinking styles which shape our mindsets and our approach to problem-solving. They also influence our relationships and our decision-making processes. In fact, studies show that the population is pretty much equally divided between these thinking styles.

4. *What are the characteristics of each of the four thinking styles?*

Before characterizing the thinking styles, it is important to realize a few basic facts:

- The distinction between the various thinking styles becomes evident early on in our lives.
- Those thinking styles are neither good nor bad. Rather, they may be either an asset or a drawback, depending on the situation and on the way we use those different thinking styles.
- The thinking styles are not rigid; most people are capable of using a mixture of styles and approaches and are not limited to a single and narrow thinking style. In fact, most people do just that.
- People are capable of learning and expanding their range of behaviors and thinking styles. In certain situations, they may even act differently and deviate from their usual manners.
- Understanding the thinking styles of others assists individuals in communication and cooperation.

Following is a daily life example of scheduling and managing a meeting, and the main priorities of individuals dominantly characterized by each of the four thinking styles:

A Logical & Analytical Self

Before the meeting:
- Goes over all the graphs, the numbers, the data, and the facts to check that there are no mistakes.
- Prepares measurable and rational arguments regarding questions that might arise.
- Prepares a presentation packed with graphs and numbers.

During the meeting:
- Presents all the data and makes sure that everyone grasps them and their significance, yet goes directly to the main issue.
- Talks about ways to implement each part of the process.
- Leads the participants in a logical way, to the required conclusions.
- Uses technical aids and gadgets throughout his presentation.
- Finishes by summarizing the technical objective that the group has to reach later on.

B Safe-Keeping & Organized Self

Before the meeting:
- Goes over schedules, what was set and what really happened.
- Reserves a meeting room of the appropriate size and place.
- Sees to the availability of the technical instruments.
- E-mails everyone about the time and place of the meeting, asking them to be on time.

During the meeting:
- Goes straight to the issue and to his presentation.
- Presents what was done as planned against what wasn't, with great accuracy and reliability.
- Finishes by setting a new schedule for the remainder of the work and by planning the different parts and areas of responsibility.

C Feeling & Relational Self

Before the meeting:
- Googles the participants of the meeting.
- Takes care of refreshments and beverages.

During the meeting:
- Throughout the meeting, uses sophisticated small talk.
- Conveys warmth and concern and makes all the present company feel good throughout the meeting.
- Empathically listens to each of the participants and asks questions to better understand the existing reality.
- Compliments the ideas of others and provides them with positive reinforcement.
- Schedules the next meeting for lunchtime.

D Explorer & Experimental Self

Before the meeting:
- Thinks about the significant accomplishments he wishes to make; prepares creative and colorful posters to assist him in conveying the main issues and convincing the participants.
- Prepares himself using a few creative, out-of-the-box solutions to problems raised at previous meetings, thus allowing the participants a choice.
- Arrives at the meeting in a good mood, full of energy.

During the meeting:
- Opens the meeting with a holistic top-to-bottom description of the current status.
- Asks questions in order to understand where the participants would like to see themselves by the end of the project.
- Uses intuition in order to promote his important concepts.
- Always finishes the meeting on an optimistic note.

5. Is it possible to map one's cognitive style or preference based on this model?

Definitely. Based on this scientific concept, Herrmann built an applied model for the evaluation of thinking styles (the HBDI).[40] The characterization of the dominant thinking style is based on a test designed to evaluate an individual's preference (or tendency) of one or more of the thinking styles associated with the four quadrants. This evaluation tool examines mental tendencies rather than competencies or skills. Still, it is known that there is a strong correlation between one's tendencies and competencies. This correlation exists because the dominance of a particular quadrant influences our interest areas, the development of our preferences and interests, our motivation and our skills.

6. How does knowing our preferences help us?

For each and every one of us, there is a unique composition of thinking styles. Understanding our personal cognitive style or preference is an asset, as it enables us to be aware of our strengths and weaknesses. This knowledge allows us to focus on the development of dormant skills, and make those available in times of need. Awareness of the various thinking styles enables us to maximize our personal skills by creating better communication with our environment and acquiring a toolset of effective learning and problem-solving techniques.

7. Is there any correlation between our occupation and our thinking style?

The profession we choose is greatly influenced by our thinking style. At the same time, the profession we choose greatly affects our thinking style. Not surprisingly, most of us choose a profession that rewards our preferences and enables us to expand our skills.

Using the HBDI survey, Herrmann created a database of about 200,000 professionals, isolating and measuring the strength of preference for each of the four thinking styles, for about 200 occupation groups. The profiles built for each of the professions indicate a **strong correlation between thinking style and work preferences.**

Engineers and economists are mostly dominant A types, but librarians and production managers are mostly B types; the dominant C type characterizes social workers, elementary school teachers, customer-service employees and volunteers; artists are mostly D types. The dominance of C-D (right-brain) characterizes counselors, psychologists and clerics. However, CEOs of large companies are mostly characterized by a tendency to evenly use three or even all four thinking styles.

8. How is the model related to the world of management?

Whether he defines himself as a leader, an executive or simply as a manager, if we look at the reality that today's manager has to face in any executive position, we will discover that he is required to use all the thinking styles, in a balanced manner.

Today's executive is required to work with diverse interfaces in his own organization and in other organizations with which he collaborates. In many cases, he has to connect with people from various countries and cultures, through various interfaces. In addition, he must work with different types of customers and retain strategic customers. Often, he is required to implement a strategy and organizational vision and to lead changes.

In order to effectively perform all his tasks, there is no doubt that one must use both the cognitive and the emotional parts of his brain. One cannot keep his good employees or his strategic customers unless he has an emotional connection with them. Graphs and schedules do not retain any of them; however, relationships based on trust and significant added value, definitely do.

9. *Can the "weaker" parts of the brain be developed?*

The "weaker" parts can most certainly be developed through awareness and training, although this is not an easy process, and one must usually invest much time and energy to achieve it.

For instance, an AB type executive, who is about to lead a change – had better not speak of facts alone (such as numbers, schedules, outputs and measures of success rates). Instead, he should address the CD type employees as well, providing answers to questions that trouble them: to what extent will the change influence their future? How does the change fit into the bigger picture? Why is there a need for change? Can they influence the process? What will be the implications for their customers? Who will be available to listen to their worries? Will they be able to personally associate themselves with the change, and how?

10. Can we talk about the four parts of the brain at the organizational level?

Organizations and their organizational cultures may be characterized according to the properties attributed to the four parts of the brain. Today, it is reasonable to assume that most organizations are dominated by the characteristics of the AB quadrants. While focusing on the bottom line, they build methodological processes based on figures, timetables, facts and projections.

Accordingly, many organizations lack a holistic approach based on leaders capable of creating an original and challenging vision, merging various ideas, taking risks and "breaking the rules." Moreover, many organizations lack managers with good interpersonal communication skills, capable of functioning well in a team, mentoring and supporting others, communicating through global interfaces within and outside the organization. In the 21st century, just like people, organizations will undoubtedly have to use all parts of their "collective brain" (the combination of its managers, employees and organizational culture) in order to reinvent themselves.

11. How is the whole brain model related to success in the 21st century?

In his book, *A Whole New Mind*, Daniel Pink characterizes today's Western society as a society on the verge of change, whose essence is a transition from the knowledge era to the conceptual era. In this new age, undoubtedly, success and even survival require adopting mindsets and approaches which are different from the ones that were prevalent so far.

The experts of knowledge will no longer be able to 'deliver the goods' on their own. In order to prosper, a wider approach will be needed, integrating all thinking styles, even those which were underestimated in the past, such as intuition and creative thinking. These qualities are expected to open new ways to handle competition in every domain.

Skills and technical knowledge will remain central aspects, but in many cases, these will be performed by computer (automated systems) and offshoring (outsourcing to lower paid employees overseas). However, executives at the head of the organizational hierarchy will have to handle wider issues, which require creativity.

Intuitive thinking and interpersonal skills, such as empathy, will be important traits in the future economy, as they will distinguish between successful and mediocre organizations. Therefore, individuals who are capable of merging various disciplines (such as observing and understanding others, creating purpose and significance, telling a story or even transforming activities into games with goals) are the ones who will become essential. Individuals, who will be wise enough to adopt the leading values of the conceptual age and to train employees with a wide creative vision, will find new opportunities and new marketing channels in the 21st century, and will determine the state of mind of modern life.

A greater complexity is being created in the organizational world as well as a built-in need for executive positions which are designed for leadership and particularly the leading of change.

These clearly call for the executives of the 21st century to use all parts of their brain, as their work has become more complex than it used to be. In fact, this is the end of the management era and the beginning of the leadership era.

In the management era, a necessary prerequisite was high-level ability (and even dominance) in the use of both parts of the left-brain. In the leadership era, at the beginning of the 21st century, an <u>additional</u> prerequisite for success is a remarkable right-brain competence, i.e. a whole-brain outstanding performance.

A leader must work with people – connect with them emotionally, create a sense of trust and empathy and make them willingly walk the extra mile for him and the organization. Many studies point to the fact that people are not actually committed to the organizations but to the managers. In his book *Motivation*,[41] Daniel Pink talks about how leaders can imbue their employees with motivation in three ways: expertise, autonomy and meaning. Without a doubt, only executives who succeed in using all four parts of the brain, will be able to do this.

In his book *The Future of Management*,[42] Garry Hamel notes that the abilities that contribute the most to the success of business organizations are passion (35%), creativity (25%) and initiative (20%). They exceed intelligence (15%) and diligence (5%). Obedience, which was also tested, makes no contribution to organizational success. It is therefore clear that organizations need leaders who can excite their employees, develop an organizational culture that encourages creativity and enable (and empower) employees to be flexible, autonomous and initiative. These leaders must use all four parts of their brain.

Another aspect of management is constantly working and

connecting with customers. In such a world where you can buy almost everything from a great number of suppliers, most products and services are a type of commodity. Therefore, highly important is the executive's ability to connect with the customers of the organization, provide them with extraordinary service and added value, build significant relationships based on trust and become a trusted advisor of strategic customers.

Another equally important aspect is leading change. To effectively lead a change, a leader must connect with his employees at the emotional level.

Successful leaders will be the ones defying the status quo, always challenging it with new concepts and ideas, and constantly recreating themselves, their staff, their department and their organization.

Questions for Mirroring and Development

Estimate to what extent are the following statements important to you at work:

1. To follow predetermined schedules
2. To hold discussion groups in which listening and sharing are possible
3. To take part in training or coaching programs
4. Before setting out on a new path:
    - To have a proof of validity and research
    - To be provided with exact and concise data
    - To have clear objectives and results presented to you
5. To learn from formal presentations and sources such as data, textbooks and bibliographies
6. To create opportunities to share emotions and to display empathy and consideration for other people's needs and emotions
7. To have a good interpersonal relationship with your superior
8. To hold team-building days for the department
9. To emphasize organization and consistency – so that each process has a beginning, a middle and an end

10. To have things predefined and accompanied with illustrations in order to facilitate their implementation
11. To have learning done through cooperation – small groups and group learning projects
12. For each process, to have a progress measurement – before and after
13. For the problem-solving process, to act in a constructive, methodological way
14. To have an opportunity to think outside the box, to experiment and to explore and discover
15. To have the possibility of working with numbers and measurable data
16. To avail yourself of the services of mentors or experts in your field of interest
17. To have opportunities to talk about the vision and how to get there

EQ Land

Questions for Thought and Reflection

Think about and explain to what extent you agree (or disagree) with the following statements:

1. The thing that influences our success the most is our Intelligence Quotient (IQ).
2. Emotional intelligence is an array of skills mostly related to interpersonal aspects.
3. Our professional and personal success is an outcome of our emotional intelligence.
4. It is impossible to significantly develop and improve emotional intelligence.
5. The concept of "emotional intelligence" is meaningless in the business world. It is only meaningful in professions like teaching, social work and medicine.
6. The concept of "emotional intelligence" pertains to the correlation between emotion and intelligence, i.e. the ability to use reason to manage emotions, and to use emotions in the thinking process.
7. A growth mindset is a necessary precondition for developing emotional intelligence.

Emotional Intelligence

"If the driving force of intelligence in twentieth-century business has been IQ, then – according to growing evidence – in the dawning twenty-first century it will be EQ, and related forms of practical and creative intelligence."

- Sawaf and Cooper

1. **What is the meaning of the concept "Emotional Intelligence"?**

The concept of Emotional Intelligence pertains to the interaction between emotion and thinking (between emotional processes and cognitive processes) and their correlation. For example, it is the ability to use sound judgment and reasoning when managing emotions, and the ability to use emotional considerations in decision-making processes.

There are a number of definitions of emotional intelligence in the professional literature. The following are two of the most prominent definitions:

- **Mayer and Salovey:** "…the ability to monitor one's own and others' feelings and emotions, to discriminate among them and to use this information to guide one's thinking and action."[43]
- **Reuven Bar-On:** "an array of personal, emotional and social competencies and skills that influence one's ability to succeed in coping with environmental demands and pressures."[44]

2. What was the basis from which this concept developed?

The idea at the basis of the concept of "Emotional Intelligence" is not a new one. Similar prior concepts, which have been studied during most of the 20th century, have their historical roots as far back as the 19th century. In fact, even in the Greek philosophy, as well as in humanistic psychology, it is possible to find debates regarding the importance of our emotions and their connection with our thought and success. Similar discussions also appear in the work published by Darwin about the contribution of emotions (and their expression) to survival.

Even though the prominent belief during the 20th century was that cognitive intelligence is the major contributor to success, the psychologist Robert Thorndike argued in 1920[45] for the existence and importance of social intelligence. According to his definition, social intelligence includes the ability to understand the emotions, the motives and the behavior of the self and others. It comprises the ability to correctly perceive the social map and to act optimally based on this information; the ability to act wisely in interpersonal relationships, to communicate and act in a synergetic manner with another individual. Even though his studies were not accepted at that time, they were the basis of the concept's development.

Twenty years later, David Wechsler, the developer of the IQ test, argued that there are more factors, or components, beyond those that exist in current evaluations of intelligence. He further argued that models of intelligence won't be complete without such components, which are important to the prediction of success.[46] Wechsler then included two such components which pertain to interpersonal skills, in his IQ test. The recognition of a wider view of intelligence thrived when Howard Gardner presented his theory of multiple intelligences, in which the interpersonal intelligence and the intra-personal intelligence were included, among others.[47] These components became the basis of emotional intelligence.

Yet, emotional intelligence is a rather new field of research, developed during the last three decades. The first researchers who dealt with this as a new field of research, and who used the term "Emotional Intelligence" were John Mayer, a professor of psychology at the University of New Hampshire, and Peter Salovey, head of the department of psychology at Yale.

By the end of the 1980s, Mayer and Salovey had published the first articles on the correlation between emotion and intelligence, areas which had been separately studied until then.[48] They continued to study the field and to validate emotional intelligence as a separate form of intelligence. The interest in the area greatly increased in 1995, with the publication of Daniel Goleman's book,[49] both as a subject for research and among the general public. Later, Daniel Goleman's article on emotional intelligence at work was selected as one of HBR's *Breakthrough Ideas for Today's Business Agenda* and as one of HBR's *10 Must Reads on Leadership*. Since then, emotional intelligence has been studied at the leading universities, and a respectable number of books and doctoral theses have been published on the subject.

3. *What are the components of Emotional Intelligence?*

Emotional intelligence is a collection of skills related to the way that emotions, behaviors and thinking interact. There are various models which use different names and present slightly different lists of components or scales. However, what is common to all of them is that they include awareness of our own emotions as well as awareness of the emotions of others, management of emotions and relationships.

The Mayer and Salovey Model

The Mayer and Salovey[50] model for emotional intelligence is a four branch model which describes the <u>abilities</u> of:

- **Perceiving Emotions:** The ability to identify one's own emotions and those of others. The ability to detect and decipher emotions in faces, pictures, voices and cultural artifacts such as art, stories or music (as well as express emotions through these). Perceiving emotions represents a basic aspect of emotional intelligence, as it makes all other processing of emotional information possible.
- **Reasoning With Emotions:** The ability to harness emotions to facilitate various cognitive activities, such as thinking, solving problems and making decisions. The emotionally intelligent person can capitalize fully upon his or her changing moods in order to best fit the task at hand.
- **Understanding Emotions**: The ability to understand emotions and emotional information, to comprehend emotion language and to appreciate complicated relationships among emotions, to recognize and describe how emotions evolve over time.

- **Managing Emotions:** The ability to regulate (manage or adapt) emotions in both ourselves and others, in order to promote emotional and intellectual growth. The emotionally intelligent person can harness emotions, even negative ones, and manage them to achieve intended goals.

The Daniel Goleman Model

Other models expanded the definition of emotional intelligence to include abilities and skills that have behavioral aspects which are also related to effective functioning. Focusing on those competencies and skills that drive leadership performance, psychologist Daniel Goleman outlined five major components:

- **Self-awareness:** The ability to recognize and understand personal moods, emotions and drives, as well as their influence on others; the ability to realistically evaluate our strengths and weaknesses. The ability to use these understandings when making decisions and solving problems.
- **Self-regulation:** The ability to manage, control and redirect our emotions (especially disruptive ones and impulses), so that they assist in achieving our goals, rather than interrupting. The ability to adapt to changing circumstances, and properly recover from emotional distress.
- **Motivation:** The ability to be driven to achieve for the sake of achievement. The strength that comes from an internal vision that guides us toward objectives which go beyond external rewards (such as money or status). The ability to initiate, take advantage of opportunities and aspire to

constant improvement, even in the face of barriers and frustrations.
- **Empathy:** The ability to understand emotions and viewpoints of others; nurturing harmony and tuning in with regard to a wide variety of individuals. The skill of treating people according to their emotional reactions and considering their feelings when making decisions.
- **Social skills:** The ability to manage relationships to move people in the desired direction. The skill of properly handling the emotions involved in relationships and accurately interpreting social situations and networks; conducting smooth interactions; using these skills to guide, negotiate, cooperate and work in teams.

The Reuven Bar-On Model

Reuven Bar-On, a clinical and organizational psychologist, devoted over 25 years to emotional intelligence research. Bar-On defined emotional intelligence as follows: "a multi-factorial array of interrelated emotional and social competencies, skills and facilitators that influence one's ability to recognize, understand and manage emotions, to relate with others, to adapt to change and solve problems of a personal and interpersonal nature, and to efficiently cope with daily demands, challenges and pressures."

As it appears from this definition, emotional intelligence includes many aspects of life. It is therefore not only necessary for efficient and effective functioning, but also highly necessary for success in life and at work.

The model developed by Reuven Bar-On describes emotional intelligence through five composite scales, which are composed of a total of 15 subscales, which were described in great detail in chapter 4.[51]

- **The Intra-Personal Component:** One's ability to be aware of his emotions, to understand them and to express them. It includes the subscales of Self-Regard, Emotional Self-Awareness, Assertiveness, Independence and Self-Actualization.
- **The Inter-Personal Component:** One's ability to be aware of the emotions of others, to understand and reflect them, to attend to others or assist them and to have good relationships. It includes the subscales of Empathy, Social Responsibility and Interpersonal Relationship.
- **Adaptability**: One's ability to adapt his emotions, thoughts and behavior to changing conditions and situations, and to cope with changes. It includes the subscales of Reality Testing, Flexibility and Problem Solving.
- **Stress Management:** One's ability to cope with his feelings in stressful situations so that they act in his favor and not against him. It includes the subscales of Stress Tolerance and Impulse Control.
- **General Mood:** One's ability to be positive and to motivate himself. It includes the subscales of Optimism and Happiness.

4. How can we measure Emotional Intelligence?

Emotional intelligence is a scientific concept, which is measurable and can be developed. There are a number of tools for measuring and evaluating emotional intelligence, among others:

MSCEIT: Together with David Caruso, Mayer and Salovey composed the first emotional intelligence test, which is referred to as a "multi-factor measurement for the evaluation of emotional intelligence," as a descendant of a previous test they had created (the MEIS). The Mayer-Salovey-Caruso Emotional Intelligence Test is an ability measure which is based on a variety of tasks, and which is designed to examine the four components of the Mayer and Salovey model.[52]

ECI: Daniel Goleman and Richard Boyatzis composed the Emotional Competence Inventory test, which examines the central aspects of Goleman's model. It also integrates self-report with the reports of others who are familiar with the subject of the evaluation (360-degree evaluation, also known as Multi-Rater Feedback). This tool is intended for the business sector and especially for management and leadership positions.[53]

EQ-i: A significant part of Bar-On's work focused on developing a measurement tool, the Emotional Quotient Inventory, which is considered a leading self-report measure of emotional intelligence. The test renders scores for the 15 subscales of the Bar-On model, the five composite scales and the total EQ score. In addition, based on built-in validity indices the test includes a correction factor which reduces potential bias and makes the test more accurate.[54]

EQ-i 2.0: This 2011 revision of the EQ-i includes some new features. This revision of the EQ-i is a continued evolution of emotional intelligence and has a greater emphasis on effectiveness in the workplace and on leadership in particular. The subscales are redefined with less overlap and all composite scales have 3 sub-scales. One major new feature is the distinction between Self-Perception and Self-Expression, which includes the new subscale of Emotional Expression. Decision Making is another new composite scale, which addresses the way in which we use emotional information in the decision making process.

5. How is Emotional Intelligence related to the business world?

Many people will argue that in order to succeed in the business world, one must not mix emotions and business. In fact, the opposite is true. A growing number of studies indicate that the intelligent use of emotions is highly necessary in order to identify problems and opportunities and in order to make better decisions.

Over 30 years ago, researchers studying effectiveness in organizations expressed concern over the fact that the widely used assessments were not good predictors of an individual's life and work success. One of the most prominent researchers, David McClelland of Harvard, believed that the ability to predict success based on academic achievements, technical skills and an impressive résumé, can be as low as 20%.

In 1973, McClelland published a revolutionary article entitled *Testing for Competence Rather than Intelligence*,[55] an article which strongly promoted the creation of a new approach to identifying excellent employees. McClelland argues that if an organization wished to hire or promote the best individual for a certain job, an executive job, for instance, it must ignore the accepted metrics.

The modern work environment and its centrality in our everyday lives creates a wide variety of emotions. The ability to successfully manage our emotional world and to act out of choice and out of a value system is crucial for success in the workplace.

Studies at various organizations have confirmed the contribution of emotional intelligence to outcomes such as employee effectiveness and productivity, through measurable operational indicators such as execution and income levels, relationships and teamwork, commitment to the workplace, stress tolerance and management skills of executives.[56]

For instance:

- In interviews with 2,000,000 employees at 700 American companies, it was found that what determined both the amount of time invested by employees and their productivity was the quality of the relationship between the employees and their superiors. It appeared that people were joining companies, but leaving managers.

- At American Express, business consultants who attended a workshop to improve their emotional intelligence increased their sales by 18.1% in comparison with a control group, which increased its sales by only 6.2%. This is an annual profit of around USD 200 million.

- At a nationwide insurance firm, it was found that insurance agents who received low scores in emotional intelligence skills such as self-confidence, initiative and empathy, sold an average amount of USD 54,000 in premiums. Those who achieved high scores, in at least five emotional intelligence subscales, sold policies with premiums of USD 114,000.
- A study focusing on a large number of professions found that salespersons endowed with high emotional intelligence were 12 times as productive as the ones at the bottom.

All over the world, a growing number of organizations now understand the business significance of recruiting employees with high emotional intelligence and of developing emotional intelligence in their existing employees. If, in the past, they would state that **the human resource** is the most important asset of an organization, today they emphasize the higher importance of **the <u>right</u> human resource**.

Emotional intelligence is especially necessary for executive positions. Executives must make many decisions, interact with a wide variety of individuals, communicate ideas, connect people to a vision and inspire them to follow. They must function in a changing environment, under stress, and lead their employees and the entire organization to success. Inter-personal and intra-personal skills are highly important for these tasks. An executive who is aware of his emotions, can successfully manage his skills and regulate them through hard times. He will be capable of understanding others, connecting with them and motivating them.

6. What motivates executives with high Emotional Intelligence?

Executives with high emotional intelligence are aware of their emotions and their thoughts in various situations. They can better understand their emotions and manage them more successfully. They have good self-regulation ability, acting by choice rather than by emotional hijacking (or *Amygdala hijacking*, the term coined by Daniel Goleman to describe emotions that inhibits a person from viewing a situation realistically).

Their awareness of their values, purpose and knowledge, enables them to set challenging yet realistic objectives and strive to attain them. They have a high sense of self-actualization and a growth mindset. They strive for constant learning and development and are not afraid of taking risks by stepping out of their comfort zone. Their ability to clearly express their opinion and their needs enables them to achieve their objectives. They are flexible and easily adapt to changes; they know how to act, even in stressful situations, to remain optimistic and happy and to communicate these feelings to their employees. They understand the emotions of others (employees, colleagues, managers and customers), recognize their needs, provide them with appropriate answers and build positive and productive relationships. They create a shared vision and successfully motivate others to join in.

Many studies have been conducted among executives. In a study by Richard Boyatzis,[57] which included over 200 executives at various levels in 12 organizations, it was shown that 14 out of the 16 skills that differentiate excellent executives from their mediocre colleagues were emotional skills. Among those were accurate self-evaluation, assertiveness, emotional self-control and organizational awareness.

In another study conducted by Hay and McBer, which included hundreds of senior executives from 15 global companies such as PepsiCo, Volvo and IBM, it was found that emotional skills were a crucial factor in differentiating between the mediocre leaders and the best leaders.[58] The best executives demonstrated significantly higher levels of emotional skills such as team leadership, political awareness, assertiveness and the drive to achieve.

McClelland surveyed data received from more than 30 different organizations about management positions in many professions, such as banking, sales and medicine.[59] This survey pointed to the fact that a wide variety of emotional skills (and a narrow range of intellectual skills) distinguished excellent executives from mediocre ones. The most significant emotional abilities were the drive to achieve (motivation), adaptability, the development of others, influencing others, assertiveness and leadership. The most significant intellectual ability was the analytical thinking.[60]

7. **What are the characteristics of executives with low Emotional Intelligence?**

Executives with low emotional intelligence tend to focus on tasks rather than on individuals. They tend neither to internalize nor to tune-in to their emotions. Low self-awareness might be the reason they are unaware of the emotions they bring to the workplace and to how they react and communicate. These executives might snap when they are upset, and hurt their employees' feelings and their sense of security. They tend to be unaware of the feelings and needs of the individuals around them and to attach little significance to them.

Such executives compromise their ability to create a sense of belonging, loyalty and commitment among their employees, and to inspire them to follow. They also spoil their ability to create a positive and happy atmosphere which is vital for satisfaction in the workplace. They find it difficult to leave their comfort zone and to effectively lead changes. Eventually, they will become irrelevant in most situations.

8. Can Emotional Intelligence be developed?

Emotional intelligence develops gradually from a young age until early adulthood.[61] Even so, it is possible to develop and improve these abilities at any stage and any age, through learning and training. Such processes deal with the identification of the individual's strengths and challenges and with focused development of skills that require improvement. These processes require will and personal engagement, as well as a commitment to invest time and effort.

Studies dealing with the evaluation of these processes in organizations indicated an increase in the emotional intelligence (as measured by such tests), as well as a rise in work effectiveness.

9. Which EI-based processes are performed by organizations?

Researchers discuss team, group and even organizational emotional intelligence. Steven Stein defines organizational emotional intelligence as the ability of an organization to reach high achievements while devoting attention to all the parties involved.[62] Many companies (such as Johnson & Johnson, Motorola, HP and American Express) conduct training processes and workshops aimed at improving certain emotional intelligence skills of their employees, as a means to increase organizational effectiveness and profits.

Such processes are usually adapted to the particular organization and its needs. They first include an inclusive assessment of the organization's needs, the challenges it faces, and an examination of its readiness for change.

The implementation stage commonly includes strategic organizational changes which are conveyed through the development programs in a variety of ways, such as lectures, workshops and personal development for managers and employees.

The implementation of such processes should involve the mobilization of the management and the creation of a leading team. They should also include proper incentives for the generation of motivation for the change, at the personal and organizational levels.

Such a process should include a long-term sustainability approach to assert the persistence of the change, including process evaluation and the examination of its effectiveness and possible improvements.

10. How is Emotional Intelligence related to success in the 21st century?

Recently, Keller & Price, two senior consultants at McKinsey, published a ground-breaking book entitled *Beyond Performances*.[63] Based on hundreds of studies, the researchers conclude that an organization that wishes to excel in the reality of the 21st century, must look beyond the business performance and put emphasis on organizational health.

Organizational health is the organization's ability to renew itself faster than the competition, in order to maintain outstanding performance over time. The writers note nine central factors through which organizations create the organizational health which is important for success in the 21st century. Among others, they mention the following factors:

- **Orientation**: A clear and significant sense among all the employees in the organization of where the organization is heading to and how it will get there.
- **Leadership:** The extent to which the leaders motivate the organization's employees.
- **Motivation:** A presence of enthusiasm which inspires individuals to make their best efforts and give their best performance, in order to accomplish tasks and achieve goals.
- **External orientation:** The quality of the relationships with customers, providers, partners and other stakeholders, in order to generate value.
- **Innovation and learning:** The quality and streamlining of new concepts, the organization's ability to adapt and shape itself when necessary.

Without a doubt, in order to create the required organizational health, organizations and their leaders will have to possess high emotional intelligence, since it is the basis of all the factors mentioned by Keller and Price.

Questions for Mirroring and Development

1. As a manager, is it important to you to express your emotions? If so, how do you express them? In which contexts?
2. Think of a situation in which you were in a good mood at work. How did your mood influence your work? How did it influence your environment?
3. To what extent would you describe yourself as an individual who often gets what he wants? How do you do it?
4. As you see it, is it important to integrate emotions into thinking processes and decision-making? Think of an example in which you did so.
5. Try to recall a situation in which you were decisive at work. What was it about? Why were you decisive in that case? What did you say? How did you say it? What did the others think?
6. Can you normally tell what other people are feeling? If so, can it help you to perform better? How?
7. As a manager, are relationships with other individuals in the organization highly significant to you?
8. To what extent would you describe yourself as someone who functions well under pressure?

9. Can you think of a case in which you formed an opinion about someone that ran counter to others' opinion, and you were right?
10. To what extent would you say that you understand organizational politics?
11. Think of a case, or period, in which you had to adapt to a change. How did you feel about the change? How did you adapt?
12. Would you describe yourself as an optimistic individual? How do you know you are one?
13. To what extent are happiness and satisfaction important to you?
14. If you could add three things to your life that would make you happier, what would they be?

Centered Leadership Land

Questions for Thought and Reflection

Think about and explain to what extent you agree (or disagree) with the following statements:

1. The significance we find at work contributes significantly to our sense of motivation and that of our subordinates.
2. The framework through which we choose to view and process the world around us influences the personal and professional outcomes in our lives.
3. People who are mostly optimistic, are more successful than pessimistic people.
4. People with strong social connections and good mentors progress faster, make more money and are more satisfied with their careers, because of their ability to forge significant relationships.
5. In order to be meaningful in an organization it is important to take chances and state your opinion clearly and unambiguously, even if it differs from the majority's opinion.
6. In order to progress, it is important for leaders to assume full responsibility for their career development and their professional development.

7. Only leaders who know how to take good emotional, physical and cognitive care of themselves, will succeed over time.

Centered Leadership

1. **What is the meaning of the term "Centered Leadership"?**

Centered leadership is a combination of five dimensions or five practices, proven to be the most important for self-actualization and success in a changing, complex and dynamic reality. The model focuses on intellectual, physical, emotional and spiritual strengths. These strengths lead executives to personal success and high professional achievements. This success inspires others and makes them want to follow their lead. It should be noted that this is not a leadership model, but rather a collection of practices that can assist anyone in leading himself, leading others and achieving greater success, in the dynamic and complex world of the 21st century.

2. **Who created the model and what is its basis?**

The centered leadership model is the product of a five-year study, in which 100 leading women executives took part through in-depth interviews, and 2,000 additional women executives participated in surveys. They included renowned CEOs in the business world, scientists, artists and executives at government offices.

Barsh and Cranston, two senior consultants at McKinsey, tried to examine what leads these executives to success.[64] They refined the results of the interviews into an impressive model which was referred to as centered leadership. This model describes the characteristics of executives who will be able to lead successfully in a changing, hyper-competitive and complex world.

3. Is this model only applicable to women executives?

Even though the model was created following a study of leading women, it is undoubtedly valid for male executives as well. As evidence, this model was adopted by two researchers from McKinsey, Keller and Price in their book *Beyond Performances*, which was mentioned in the chapter on emotional intelligence.[65] When discussing the issue of leadership, the writers follow the centered leadership model and describe its contribution to the success of managers, regardless of gender.

The book deals with the ways to achieve business and organizational excellence in a reality that is very different from that of the 20th century. The authors present an extensive model, based on in-depth interviews and the analysis of hundreds of studies conducted at organizations. They conclude that in the complex and uncertain 21st century, many organizations will disappear because they are incapable of managing effective change processes. Only organizations that are capable of **integrating performance, focus and organizational health**, will succeed over time. That remains true regardless of the gender of the organization's managers.

4. What are the components of the model?

The model is composed of five dimensions. Their integration provides organization leaders with the endurance and emotional abilities required for continuous self-improvement, as well as organizational improvement.

When the five dimensions of centered leadership are put

together, they enable people to achieve their goals in life and at work through a clear sense of destination, belonging, stamina and control. Centered leaders feel they can lead constant changes in the organization and make the most out of any challenge or opportunity.

A survey conducted by McKinsey among 1,147 senior executives found that the executives who noted that they are characterized by four or five of these dimensions, had high levels of passion for work, were effective leaders and were satisfied with their lives. It was also found that the five dimensions reinforce each other.

These are the five dimensions and their characteristics:

Meaning: discovering who we are and what we were meant to do

Typically, leaders who rank high on this dimension, feel highly committed to their work and strive to achieve their goals out of passion and enthusiasm. They are aware of their strengths, use them and inspire others to act likewise. Contrarily, an executive who lacks a sense of meaning, will live his life from one weekend to another.

It was also found that a sense of meaning is closely correlated with happiness and energy. In fact, the contribution of this dimension to general satisfaction with life is five times higher than that of other dimensions. The explanation is simple: the sense of meaning makes us participate in activities we enjoy, using our strengths. We experience a sense of accomplishment, and our work, even if it is difficult and challenging, invokes energy instead of draining it. The contribution of a sense of meaning to happiness is widely supported in research. In one of the most prominent studies, Sonja Lyubomirsky noted that finding meaning is the safest way to increase the individual's level of happiness in the long run.[66]

In addition to the positive implications of the dimension of meaning at the personal level, it also has an organizational contribution: when leaders find meaning and feel connected to the activities related to their goals, they generate positive energy around them and inspire others. The sense of meaning experienced by the staff increases their motivation and productivity in a way that cannot be achieved through formal incentives or a sanction system. Thus, the contribution of meaning is cyclic: as leaders contribute to a cause larger than themselves – to other individuals in the organization or to the organization itself – their sense of meaning grows stronger, and they are more inspiring to others.

Positive framing: finding opportunities in difficulties, seeing difficult problems in a way that encourages creative solutions and innovation

The infrastructure through which we choose to view and interpret the world influences our personal and professional achievements. It is important to note that "positive framing" does not mean putting on a pair of rose-colored glasses, but the ability to see the facts as they are and still emphasize the positive. Executives who positively frame their reality can bring their team to feelings of capability and ability, instead of submission and helplessness.

Pessimistic people tend to see negative situations as constant, broad-ranging and self-derived. This limits their thinking, preventing them from bringing forth strategic concepts, since it drains their energies. On the other hand, optimistic people see negative situations as temporary, distinct and external. This enables them to see the situation with greater objectivity and act quickly.

Optimistic people, who naturally choose to focus on the opportunities of each situation, have higher success rates, in comparison with pessimistic individuals, who focus on the negatives. Although we are not all born optimistic, studies do indicate that our observation of life is only half innate. Studies presented by Seligman in his book *Learned Optimism*[67] indicates that people can acquire tools used by optimistic individuals when viewing situations. The optimism, whether natured or nurtured, underlies the ability of leaders to be flexible and to recuperate: to take blows, evaluate their implications and respond in an appropriate, effective manner.

However, it is important to maintain a balance between optimism and a fair sense of perspective and reality testing, as positive framing can neither be achieved in all situations nor at all times.

Connecting with others: being part of a group, growing, developing and achieving together

This dimension relates to the ability to create meaningful relationships with people of different groups. Studies indicate that people who have strong social networks and good mentors tend to progress faster, make more money and be more satisfied with their careers. This means that creating meaningful relationships is part of a leader's everyday job.

Successful leaders build complex networks of connections, which increase their personal influence and accelerate their development, thanks to the variety of ideas and the experience they are exposed to through these connections. As to such a network of influential people, it isn't restricted to the list of the organization's senior executive. It also includes lower rank key employees, who are not necessarily managers. Exposure to lower rank employees and the benefits of this exposure, are what Jack Walsh terms "reverse mentoring."

As a rule, relationships are essential to both our emotional well-being and success. People who invest in their relationships, find that others are willing to assist them and to support their wishes, thus making them more successful as leaders.

Engaging: finding our voice, showing courage, holding our own opinions and taking advantage of opportunities in spite of all the risks

Engagement means commitment, involvement and proactive behavior. It is closely related to risk-taking and assuming responsibility for our actions. It's the understanding that we are responsible and that we can influence our organizational environment, unlike passiveness and the feeling that everything is out of our control.

Engaged leaders enjoy a sense of capability; they act with determination in order to achieve their objectives. Engaging is different from positive framing: while positive framing enables us to see opportunities, engagement grants us the courage to try: to take advantage of the opportunities we identified, without fear. Committed executives take chances and express their opinions and desires clearly and unambiguously, even if it contradicts the opinion of the majority. These leaders also assume full responsibility for their career development and professional progress. Generally, these are leaders who are willing to leave their fancy offices and assist in solving necessary operational issues.

Energizing: *methodically investing in physical, mental and emotional energy and creating actions and habits necessary to stimulate energy in other individuals*

Each person has a limited amount of energy, from the CEO in his fancy office down to the most junior employee. The challenging reality in which we are living calls for massive amounts of energy on a daily basis. In addition, constant improvement requires enthusiasm and commitment from many individuals within the organization. For this to be possible, leaders must know how to preserve their own energy and that of others, and avoid the exhaustion of their resources.

It is known that executives and senior employees work hard, and a significant part of them are unable to achieve a balance between their jobs and their lives outside work. However, awareness of the fact that we have to do it, for ourselves as managers and for our employees, can promote us toward better life habits.

Individuals who are occupied with what they love and what they are good at, maintain high energy levels. When we use our core skills – our strengths – in order to overcome challenges and achieve goals, we experience a mental state in which our work is perceived as effortless. As a result, we have better output, higher productivity and greater satisfaction from our work. This mental state was defined and called "flow" by psychologist Mihaly Csikszentmihalyi.[68]

How can we experience flow? Typically, by doing a job that we love and which is within our abilities. Thus, when we face challenging objectives that involve using our skills, we can focus on the task at hand and devote our best efforts to it, while requiring less energy to do so.

However, it is important to remember that sometimes, even though we are focused, capable and motivated, we might also fail on a task. In general, our ability to easily recover from failure attests to our stamina and adaptability, as a constant process of improvement is a fundamental characteristic of leadership. Our ability to recover and re-enlist our energies is dependent on the other four dimensions of the centered leadership model – awareness of what is significant to us (the passions and strengths that will help us succeed); maintaining a positive point of view; connecting with our social networks; courageous involvement and the willingness to face risks head on.

5. Which Centered Leadership related processes are performed by organizations?

Organizations are performing quite a few processes to strengthen the five dimensions, even if they are unaware of them. For instance, the implementation of programs related to social responsibility is related to the sense of organizational meaning. So does the embedding of a vision and values. Training and 'Trusted Advisor' programs are related to the dimension of connecting with others. Attempts to build Work-Life Balance programs are related to the dimension of energy creation.

The most challenging dimension, which many organizations find hard to handle, is the dimension of engagement, as fewer employees and executives feel a personal connection or commitment to the organizations in which they work. Such employees and executives may not truly assume full responsibility for various processes in the organization.

6. How is the Centered Leadership model related to the 21st century?

Even though the five dimensions have always been important to the success of executives, nowadays, the dynamic, demanding, complex and competitive reality takes many executives to the outer limits of their abilities. This is why each of the dimensions, and all of them combined, are important for the survival and success of executives and organizations.

Adopting the centered leadership model changes the point of view of executives and makes them focus on their personal responsibility for shaping their own future. If in the 20th century executives were more passive, and would often tell themselves "the organization is going to worry about my career plan" or "the organization is going to notify me of my responsibilities" and so on, the centered leadership model places the brunt of the responsibility on the shoulders of the executive aspiring to lead. Leaders who know how to be proactive and use these five dimensions will continue to succeed over time. Those who do not – will disappear.

When it comes to leading a change process, an executive who sets out devoid of energy, is guaranteed not to make it effectively through the change. Leaders who know how to take care of themselves and their energy levels will undoubtedly succeed in managing others in the white water.

7. Can the various dimensions of the model be developed?

Certainly, everyone who wants to develop those skills can do it. The dimensions described above are based on emotional intelligence skills. This is why an executive with high capabilities within relevant emotional intelligence skills can turn any dimension into an action plan and start developing it. If he lacks these skills, he must develop the relevant "muscles" first and only then set up a plan for action.

For instance, if a manager has good interpersonal skills, he should build a program to strengthen and preserve his social network within as well as outside the organization – decide who are the most significant individuals for the process, and what he is going to do about each of them (sending e-mails, having lunch, providing assistance, planning a shared project).

Later on, he can even get closer to a senior manager and ask him to be his mentor.

When it comes to strategic customers, he should set up a program to become their trusted advisor: to build a close relationship based on trust and extraordinary professional skills.

Another example has to do with involvement and responsibility. If the skills of independence, assertiveness and self-evaluation are the executives' strengths and do not require development, he can identify meaningful issues in the organization that are in need of improvement and take responsibility for them. Often, these are processes that no one in the organization is willing to take on, and they present an opportunity for such an executive.

Later on, during meetings, the executive can consciously decide what significant messages he wants to communicate and phrase them clearly. He can use a sympathetic and emphatic description of his opinions and ideas, even when these are different from those of others. An interesting paradox is that even though most people do not like it when they hear different opinions, most of them can value these opinions when expressed properly and reliably by individuals who are perceived as trustworthy and responsible, who know where to lead the team and who are capable of leading it.

Questions for Mirroring and Development

1. Do you know why you have chosen your career?
2. Have you ever asked yourself, "Is this what I want to keep on doing?" and answered "Yes!"?
3. Are you doing a job that expresses your strengths?
4. Do you have a sense of purpose in your job?
5. Are you investing worthy effort in nurturing and maintaining your social network?
6. Do you have a mentor with whom you can consult, and who cares about your development?
7. Are you providing added value to the individuals around you (subordinates, colleagues, superiors, customers)?
8. Do you take full responsibility for your career development?
9. Are you aware of your voice and are you making it heard?
10. Have you achieved most of your ambitions so far?
11. Are you capable of balancing your work and your personal life? Are you actually doing it?
12. Do you have enough activities that bring pleasure to your life?

13. Are you getting enough sleep, eating healthy food and exercising?
14. Are you spending enough time with people who "charge your energy"?
15. Are you celebrating personal and organizational success?

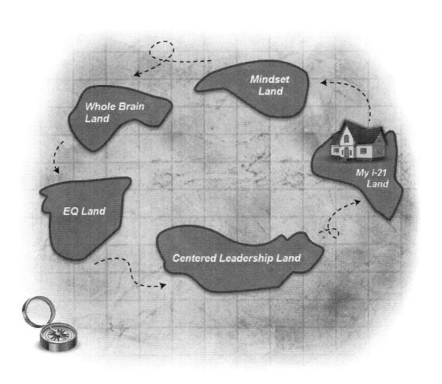

I Have a Dream

I dream of employees and executives coming to work every morning with a sense of meaning and pleasure.

Those who understand that all the things that have happened so far, do not necessarily predict what's in store; who see where the world is heading and take full responsibility for their career development and their personal value proposition;

Who are courageous enough to leave their comfort zone even before something or someone makes them do so;

Who understand that their personal and organizational success relies on all parts of their brain and never undervalue any part of it;

Who have respect for the soft skills and their importance in their interaction with their employees, peers and customers, and understand that the way to achieve perfect performance is through those soft skills;

Who are not afraid to talk about emotions and who can use their emotions wisely in order to motivate themselves and their employees;

Who build complex networks of connections and relationships, increase their personal influence and accelerate their development;

Who are capable of seeing the harsh facts of life yet accentuating the positive and creating a sense of optimism in themselves, their friends, their staff and even their superiors;

Who support themselves and can maintain themselves emotionally, physically and cognitively, and balance their private and professional lives;

Who find profound meaning in their work and strive to realize their objectives out of passion and enthusiasm;

Who understand that what matters the most are training, development and growth, and are willing to invest their time and effort in order to succeed;

And most important – who are clear on the real important things in life.

Without a doubt, employees and executives who get there, will experience their share of success during the first decades of the 21st century!

Sources

1. Daniel Pink, *A Whole New Mind: Why Right-Brainers Will Rule the Future*, Riverhead Trade, 2006.
2. Steve Tappin and Andrew Cave, *The Secrets of CEOs: 150 Global Chief Executives Lift the Lid on Business, Life and Leadership*, Nicholas Brealey Publishing, 2008.
3. Steve Tappin and Andrew Cave, *The NEW Secrets of CEOs: 200 Global Chief Executives on Leading*, Nicholas Brealey Publishing, 2010.
4. Rosabeth Moss Kanter, *SuperCorp: How Vanguard Companies Create Innovation, Profits, Growth, and Social Good*, Crown Business, 2009.
5. Daniel Pink, *A Whole New Mind: Why Right-Brainers Will Rule the Future*, Riverhead Trade, 2006.
6. The Center for Creative Leadership (CCL®) is a global provider of executive education that develops better leaders through its exclusive focus on leadership education and research.

7   Carol Dweck, *Mindset: The New Psychology of Success*, Ballantine Books, 2007.

8   Howard Gardner, *Frames of Mind: The Theory of Multiple Intelligences*, Basic Book, 1983.

9   Robert Sternberg, *Successful Intelligence: How Practical and Creative Intelligence Determine Success in Life*, Plume, 1997.

10 Malcolm Gladwell, *Outliers*, Little, Brown, and Company, 2008.

11 Ibid., 7.

12 John P. Kotter, *Leading Change: An Action Plan from the World's Foremost Expert on Business Leadership*, Harvard Business Press, 1996.

13 Ned Herrmann, The Whole Brain Business Book: Unlocking the Power of whole Brain Thinking in Organizations and Individuals, McGraw-Hill, 1996.

14 Susie Weller, *Meet the Four Thinking Styles: Which One Best Describes You?* (adapted from Herrmann International, see www.hbdi.com).

15 Adapted from a white paper by Michael Morgan and Ann Nehdi titled, *Know Change or No Change Will Happen* (the white paper is available on the Herrmann International Website at www.hbdi.com).

16 Spencer Johnson, *Who Moved My Cheese*, Vermilion, 1999.

17 Reuven Bar-On, *The Bar-On Emotional Quotient Inventory (EQ-i): Technical Manual*, Multi-Health Systems, 1997.

18 Peter Salovey and John D. Mayer, *"Emotional Intelligence,"* in Imagination, Cognition and Personality 9 (3), 1989, pp. 185–211.

19 Daniel Goleman, *Emotional Intelligence: Why it Can Matter More than IQ*, Bantam Books, 1995.
20 Moshe Zeidner, Gerald Matthews, Richard D. Roberts, *What We Know about Emotional Intelligence: How It Affects Learning, Work, Relationships, and Our Mental Health*, A Bradford Book, 2012.
21 Roberts, R.D., Zeidner, M., & Matthews, G. (2001). *Does emotional intelligence meet traditional standards for an intelligence? Some new data and conclusions*. Emotion, 1, pp.196–231.
22 Larry Bossidy and Ram Charan, *Execution: The Discipline of Getting Things Done*, Random House Business Books, 2002.
23 Reuven Bar-On, *The Bar-On Emotional Quotient Inventory (EQ-i): A Test of Emotional Intelligence*, Multi-Health Systems, 1997.
24 *The Future of Enterprise*, World Economic Forum, Davos Annual Meeting, 2011.
25 Joanna Barsh, Susie Cranston and Geoffrey Lewis, How Remarkable Women Lead: The Breakthrough Model for Work and Life, Crown, 2009.
26 Scott Keller and Colin Price, Beyond Performance: How Great Organizations Build Ultimate Competitive Advantage, John Wiley and Sons, 2011.
27 Barsh, J. & De Smet, A., *Centered leadership through the crisis: McKinsey survey results*, McKinsey Quarterly, October 2009.
28 Barsh, J., Mogelof, J. & Webb, C., *The value of centered leadership: McKinsey Global Survey Results*, McKinsey & Company, New York, 2010.

29 Csikszentmihalyi, M., *Flow: The Psychology of Optimal Experience*, New York: Harper and Row, 1990.

30 Ibid. 7.

31 Ibid. 7.

32 Ibid. 12.

33 John P. Kotter, *A Sense of Urgency*, Harvard Business School Publishing, 2008.

34 Ibid. 27, p. 177.

35 Harvard Business Review Staff, *How Companies Can Profit from a "Growth Mindset"*, Harvard Business Review, November 2014, pp. 28-32.

36 Gary Hamel and C. K. Prahalad, *Competing for the Future*, Harvard Business Review Press, 1994.

37 Howard Gardner, *Changing Minds: The Art and Science of Changing Our Own and Other People's Minds*, Harvard Business School, 2004.

38 Ned Herrmann, *The Whole Brain Business Book: Unlocking the Power of whole Brain Thinking in Organizations and Individuals*, McGraw-Hill, 1996.

39 Herrmann Brain Dominance Instrument. In Wikipedia: The Free Encyclopedia. Wikimedia Foundation Inc. Encyclopedia on-line. Retrieved 2 February 2015. Available from http://en.wikipedia.org/wiki/Herrmann_Brain_Dominance_Instrument. Internet.

40 HBDI: the Herrmann Brain Dominance Instrument, Herrmann International.

41 Daniel H. Pink, *Drive: The Surprising Truth About What Motivates Us*, Penguin Group US, 2009.

42 Gary Hamel, *The Future of Management*, Harvard Business Review Press, 1997.
43 Peter Salovey and John D. Mayer, *"What is emotional intelligence?"* - in Peter Salovey and David Sluyter (eds.), *Emotional Development and Emotional Intelligence: Educational Implications*, Basic Books, 1997, pp. 3-31.
44 Ibid. 15.
45 Richard K. Thorndike, *Intelligence and Its Uses*, Harper's Magazine 140, 1920, pp. 227-335.
46 David Wechsler, "*Non-intellective Factors in General Intelligence*," Psychological Bulletin 37, 1940, pp. 444-445.
47 Howard Gardner, *Multiple Intelligences: The Theory in Practice*, Basic Books, 1993.
48 Ibid. 16.
49 Ibid. 17.
50 Ibid. 35.
51 Ibid. 20.
52 Peter Salovey, John D. Mayer, and David R. Caruso, "*Mayer-Salovey-Caruso Emotional Intelligence Test (MSCEIT)*," Multi-Health Systems, 2002.
53 Richard E. Boyatzis, Daniel Goleman, Kenneth Rhee, "*Clustering competence in emotional intelligence: Insights from the Emotional Competence Inventory (ECI)s*" In Reuven Bar-On and James D. A. Parker (eds.), *Handbook of emotional intelligence*, Jossey-Bass, 2000, pp. 343-362.
54 Reuven Bar-On, "*The Bar-On Model of Emotional-Social Intelligence (ESI)*" Psicothema 17, 2005, pp. 1-29.

55 David C. McClelland, "*Testing for Competence rather than for 'Intelligence'*", American Psychologist 28(1), 1973, pp. 1-14.

56 Reuven Bar-On, "*The Bar-On Model of Emotional Intelligence: A valid, Robust and Applicable EI model*", Organizations and People, 14, 2007, pp. 27-34.

57 Richard E. Boyatzis, *The Competent Manager: A Model for Effective Performance*, John Wiley and Sons, 1982.

58 Hay and McBer Research and Innovation Group (1997), quoted in: Daniel Goleman, *Working with Emotional Intelligence*, Bantam, 1998.

59 David C. McClelland, "*Identifying Competencies with Behavioral Event Interviews*", Psychological Science 9(5), 1998, pp. 331-339.

60 Cary Cherniss and Daniel Goleman, "*The Emotionally Intelligent Workplace: How to Select For, Measure, and Improve Emotional Intelligence in Individuals, Groups, and Organizations*", Wiley, 2001.

61 Carolyn Saarni, "*The development of Emotional Competence: Pathways for Helping Children to Become Emotionally Intelligent*", in R. Bar-On, J. G. Maree, & M. J. Elias (eds.), *Educating people to be emotionally intelligent*, Praeger, 2007, pp. 15-36.

62 Steven Stein, *Make Your Workplace Great: The 7 Keys to an Emotionally Intelligent Organization*, Jossey-Bass, 2007.

63 Scott Keller and Colin Price, *Beyond Performance: How Great Organizations Build Ultimate Competitive Advantage*, John Wiley and Sons, 2011.

64 Joanna Barsh, Susie Cranston and Geoffrey Lewis, *How

Remarkable Women Lead: The Breakthrough Model for Work and Life, Crown, 2009.

65 Ibid. 54.

66 Sonja Lyubomirsky, *The How of Happiness: A New Approach to Getting the Life You Want*, Penguin Group US, 2007.

67 Martin Seligman, *Learned Optimism: How to Change Your Mind and Your Life*, Random House, 1990.

68 Ibid. 24.